OUR BIBLICAL HERITAGE

OUR BIBLICAL HERITAGE

*

The *Way* in Ancient China and The West

The Lectio Press

in association with

Ashgrove Publishing

London & Bath

CONTENTS

Publisher's Introduction / 7

Part I

The Family of The Way and The Grace of God

Chapter One
The Background of Scripture / 11

Chapter Two
The Scene of Companionship / 13

Chapter Three
The Translation Process / 15

Chapter Four
The Ideographic Approach / 19

Chapter Five
The Alphabetical Approach / 35

Chapter Six
Points of Similarity / 37

Appendices / 39

CONTENTS

Part II

The Written Companionship of *The Holy Bible*

Chapter Seven
The Librarial Structure of *The Holy Bible* / 65

Chapter Eight
The Pentateuch / 67

Chapter Nine
The Septuagint – The Kingdom / 69

Chapter Ten
The Septuagint – Prophecy / 75

Chapter Eleven
Gospel / 79

Chapter Twelve
The Church / 81

Chapter Thirteen
The Revelation / 83

Epilogue / 85 **Acknowledgements** / 87

Publisher's Introduction

With the increasing complexity of modern life many are finding an ever widening gap between the counsels of religion and the effects of technological change. Moreover modern telecommunications, the 'media', have contributed to a confused sea of changing values.

The oldest and most stable influence has always been that of holy writ yet even here there seems to be a feeling of distance from day to day living and this gap has not significantly been closed simply by translation into modern language.

There is a need to take stock of the way we look at scripture and of all that can be known about its underlying process of growth. This study looks at new information to see how scriptural composition came to address the self as a whole, independent of change. The intention is to keep to orthodoxy whilst revising evaluation of the literary material available.

Without trespassing upon the territory of religion it is practicable to approach our biblical heritage on the basis of companionship with the reader.

PART I

The Family of The Way and The Grace of God

Chapter One

The Background of Scripture

There are several families of scripture but this account deals with one only, the family of The Way and The Grace of God, which is best known in the western world in its completed library, *The Holy Bible*.

The first thing to be said about it is that it came into being to accompany life of dedication. The second is that it advanced to its final form through a series of cumulative editions, each reflecting the authority of the living stage of advance.

Of scripture as the word of prophecy Saint Peter wrote that it is more sure than any interpretation because it was spoken by holy men of God, moved by The Holy Spirit (*2 Peter* 1:21). It is not generally realized that scripture is set apart from other literature not only by its content and authority but also by the way it was composed to accompany inner man.

This would very likely remain indefinitely unrealized were it not for the fact that another library belongs to the same family. Only recently could the fact have come to light since the linking text was published in translation in 1949.

The Way and The Grace of God are called *Dao* and *De* in Chinese. Most of the texts had been translated in the nineteenth century, when they had their western vogue more as a curio than a contribution to civilization.

The present significance of the connection is that in the

Chinese texts are to be found the ground rules of the methodology of written companionship. Arising from this companionship is an implicit view of the self of the reader, a view which, though formed through the inner life is extractable for outside use.

Anciently, scripture was reserved to dedicants and only read aloud to lay folk. Of course it became the continuity of religious observance but it also entered canon of outer civilization by being centrally archived. In this way it acquired lay literary status, but without the original purpose. In this status its methodology of companionship has been glossed and its implication is missed.

That literary companionship with the life of dedication to The Way and The Grace of God should have been prepared both in the Middle East and in China in ancient times is a matter of record. The underlying physical link was that of the trade routes by land and sea, in which silk and gold were probably the key products of barter, with jade and gems a close second. In the West it is now known that the earliest scriptural center of the tradition was in Mesopotamia, between the Tigris and Euphrates.

This accounts for the separate branches of development, the Eastern remaining in sinic characters, the Western entering alphabetical Hebrew then Greek and Latin.

There is one other consideration. From very early times scripture was so twinned as to match active and passive ways of dedication, a fact which also leads towards transcendence in the personal examples which are the landmarks of scriptural advance.

Chapter Two

The Scene of Companionship

A short cut to the partnership between reader and script is provided by the old riddle, as to which of the chicken and the egg came first. For at the very base of inspection of the life of dedication is the co-presence in individuality of Divine mystery and grace. Human awareness of these as ultimate antipodes of being enters registration through mind and nature of soul but application through activity and passivity. So if the self is described as the tension of relationship between God and individuality there is organism of reciprocity and interaction having meaning and purpose. In the West this concept reached to the Godhead but in the East to Supreme Absoluteness.

Companionship within the tension indicated inner and outer centers of identity so that, with mystery and grace, there was perceived to be quaternity of soul, co-existent with unity of life and centrality of individual self. Companionship had to be implemented through process of reciprocity and system of interaction, the one resembling a ladder and the other a schematic design. Therefore the dynamics of reciprocity paralleled the statics of interaction, and so it was with reading of scripture.

The composition of scripture had therefore to emulate both the inspiration and the accordance of companionship with God. Yet it also had to be translated into imagery capable of intertranslation between external and internal recognitions.

In both East and West the antipodes of recognition were named Heaven and Earth of Divinity and were projected upon Humanity as pneuma and soma. That is overt in the Chinese texts but has to be verified in the Hebrew and Christian, in which the compositorial mechanics are taken for granted. The implication is present throughout the literary structure of *The Holy Bible*.

What has to be allowed for is that the translators of scripture worked according to linguistic priorities rather than original compositorial methodology, of which they would have been unaware. There is consequently some inconsistency of terminology, though not to the extent of obscuring inner truth. In any case languages tend to be idiosyncratic.

It follows that in the approach to the literary structure of companionship there have to be four stages. The first is simply acknowledgment of a single underlying tradition of dedication to Divine Mystery and Grace. Secondly, though not at all simply, Eastern and Western approaches have to be fitted together before further examination. Next a view has to be gained of the self implied by the companionship. Finally there has to be sight of how scripture accompanies personal integration.

Chapter Three

The Translation Process

The situation in regard to reconciliation of the two branches of scripture of the tradition of The Way and The Grace of God is that, since the Chinese texts of companionship had been assumed to be a version of philosophy, there had been stalemate. In reality the outward view of the literature was not complemented by the inner view. Furthermore the *Dao* stream texts were taken to emanate from within one religion and the *De* stream texts from another. It was not realized that they accompanied passive and active ways of dedication of life.

Historically speaking the Chinese texts had been archived in the Imperial Library, where they were treated as national heritage at the levels of civilization, culture and religions. To ordinary folk their place was assured, because of tradition and piety, in that they had been written by Sages.

Academically speaking, despite recognition of well defined anthologies there was none of coherent library of dedication.

The first translations were into Latin by Jesuit missionaries in the seventeenth and eighteenth centuries. These were followed by others, in French, German and English, during the nineteenth century, the bulk having been achieved by the Scottish missionary James Legge DD, working from Hong Kong.

Not until the American translation of the last of the three

Huang Di texts, published in 1949, could it have been apparent that these three constituted an anthology central to active and passive streams and particularly to the literature ascribed to the Four Sages.

The translation process did not extend to the collation of a library compatible with *The Holy Bible* although it did show strong similarities in methodology and figuration. For this reconciliation it is necessary to look at biblical structure, to which the key is the successive cumulative anthologies of *Genesis* (Chaldean and Hebrew introduction), the Pentateuch, the Septuagint and the Vulgate. Since China did not aspire to prophecy its level is that of The Law and Kingdom.

On return to the texts of *Dao* and *De* as a single library of dedication the translated texts group themselves as:

1. The Huang Di library.
2. The *Yi* and *Li* of the Sages.
3. The Five Classics of Confucius.
4. The Four Teaching Texts in active and passive streams.

From the aspect of approach to dedication, however, the first two stages are analytical of companionship and introductory of Antiquity. The second two are for companionship and identification with Kingdom in Antiquity.

There remains the matter of translation of the Vulgate. The essentials of this story are that in the 14th, 15th and 16th centuries there were several English (and German) translations and revisions, resulting in the Authorized or King James Version published in 1611. This, more than any other, appears to have caught the spirit of continuity in companionship. After 1870 and particularly in the 20th century a number of differing versions have appeared, each having a slight change of emphasis away from inner companionship in favour of outer (supposed) accessibility.

It is worth recalling that the Vulgate itself, which incorporates the Greek Septuagint and Greek translations of the Apostolic texts, was prepared some three centuries after the incarnation of Jesus; with the authority of the Pope, the backing of Saint Augustine of Hippo and the work of Saint Jerome in the Syrian desert and at Bethlehem. There is strong indication that the compositorial methodology of the tradition of dedication to The Way and The Grace of God was taken into account.

Chapter Four

The Ideographic Approach

The Chinese language is not spelled but makes use of the ideograph, which is a direct depiction of a combined sight/sound context, so that it lends itself to the passage of parallel meanings. Secondly the culture of China is unimpaired, unlike that of the Mediterranean. Thirdly specific texts exist called Classics, which were designed to correlate with reader functioning. These were termed *jing*. Such is the way of the language that the homophonic meaning of *jing* is a well. So a Classic not only accompanied its reader but modeled the accompaniment as determined by dedicant experience.

That the outside world understands little of the life of dedication to God is true everywhere. It is often mistaken for religion and tends to be judged according to secular attitudes. Chinese scripture, which had been lodged with the Imperial Library by decree, was sacred to the culture. So, before Buddhist penetration, the external religious observance of the culture had divided into so-called Confucianism and Daoism. In reality, as their appropriated texts reveal, both religious streams owed their origin to the centrality of Huang Di.

Parallelism of scriptural companionship, also manifest in the scriptures of Christianity, is a reflection of the co-presence of nature and mind in the reader; to each of which Divinity is at once both mysterious and manifest. So there is an outward tendency to specialize according to either approach. So-called Daoism followed the route of the inner nature whilst its counter part reasoned along the lines of benevolence and righteousness.

The reality of the reconstituted core scriptural library is otherwise. The outermost layer consists of four teaching texts, forming a frame which combines parallelism with inner:earlier and outer:later presentation of the other two layers. The four texts are ascribed to:

1. Lao Zi (Old Master)
2. Zhuang Zi
3. The disciples of Gong Fu Zi.
4. The disciples of Meng Zi.

Texts 1 and 2 address the inner and outer nature of soul whilst 3 and 4 address the inner and outer mind of soul. Upon analysis their common jargon is extensive and all address centrality to Dao (The Way) and De (The Grace) of God as exemplified in Antiquity.

The four texts, to be examined in greater detail later, also acknowledge two key points of Divine relationship with the self, Superior Man and The Sage.

From the teaching anthology it is easiest to pass directly to the head anthology of centrality, antiquity and empire of self. These three texts are ascribed to Huang Di (this title meaning inwardly Central Authority but outwardly Yellow Emperor).

Centrality – Divine Covenant

The first text (*yin fu jing*, see Appendix A) treats Divine relationship with individuality as a contract or covenant and proceeds to model its operation in mystical, spiritual and developmental tiers, showing their interrelation. In the mystical context the key constituents are Heaven and pneuma, the fivefold mechanism of mind, the heart as the wellspring of nature, the observable Creation and the nature as a central State under The Sage. The spiritual context is founded upon inner rest in God in absolute stillness. Around this occurs interaction with functioning, whereby nourishment is drawn from Divinity and transformed into integrative activity in soul towards the building of Superior Man (higher self). This process is translated for outward perception as Divine Ordinance. Finally the developmental tier deals with seven aspects of Divine companionship. These are: complementation of inner with outer; heart, nature and Divine mercy; central purity of nature in soul; immortality; balance in self and individual choice; self-regulation and health; wisdom and understanding. Two key tenets are that there is a spring of Divine power in the heart and that the spring of life is in the eyes.

Antiquity – Descent in Myth and Legend

The second Huang Di text (*zu shu nian*, *Annals of The Bamboo Books*, see Appendix C) is not a *jing* but a set of annals depicting five dynasties later known as the times of the Ancient Kings. In it myth and legend are so interwoven as to yield parallelism of dominance and regimen in what is a portrait in analytical terms of the scriptural course of The Fall from Divine grace of relationship. On the one hand myth addresses nature and arrives at similarities of sound association. On the other the Divine Day passes from light into cycle and arrives through figures and words at the drainage of land and the standard of measure according to length and intensity of shadow.

Annals of The Bamboo Books thus constitutes unique linkage between the upper levels of soul and the individual self in tension between the Right Way and the Way of Peace. Rather than act as companionship the text sketches the principles of annalistic composition.

Empire of Self – Divine Dialogue

The third Huang Di text (*nei jing su wen*, see Appendix D) is a dialogue between the Yellow Emperor and an editorial figure named Chi Bo. More than a *jing*, it is an Inner Classic (*nei jing*). Although no literary accountancy for that distinction is available the status probably emphasizes that it deals with inner healing of body.

In principle the text models a 'heart' set between heavenly vitality and earthly health. The 'heart' combines coalescence of identity with pulsating organization. The character of the text is set by the use of physical organic functioning (as then understood) as analogy for the operation of soul.

In outline the dialogue is an analysis of an 'earlier' Divine Empire of nine provinces which is outwardly encompassed by a 'later' Human Empire of twelve provinces, bordering on the circumstantial. This dual organization (see the figure below) strengthens a reference to Relational Number in the Bamboo

Annals, expanding the scriptural compositorial discipline which that provides.

Earlier Empire	Later Empire
1 The Fall from Grace	1 Unity of Head and Members
2 The Foundation of Soul	2 Reciprocity
3 Enumeration of The Good	3 Health
4 The Will to Healing	4 Soul
5 The Pulsating Organisation	5 Viscera
6 Universe of Life and Death	6 Bowels
7 The Modulation of Relationship	7 Female Reproductivity
8 The Creation for Service	8 Male Reproductivity
9 Human Desire and Perfect Peace	9 Apertures of Relationship
	10 Left and Right Branching
	11 Concordance of Contentment and Desire
	12 Ducting of Vital Essence

We now come to the literature linking inward centrality to outward teaching. It is ascribed to the Four Sages of China, namely King Tai, King Wen, the Duke of Zhou and Confucius. Here the picture is less immediately clear cut since considerable consolidation took place under the Fourth Sage. From various references the picture emerges of two principal stages, the formulation of Divine Archetypes and Ceremonials and the composition of *The Five Classics*. These stages are amplifications of specific central teachings and are associated with development out of Central State into Middle Kingdom. The standpoints of the first three Sages are those of upper, middle and lower Antiquity whilst the Fourth Sage wrote from an impartial setting, that of Lu State outside the Bamboo Annals.

As to the formulatory texts the archetypal have not been preserved whilst the ceremonial have. Nevertheless the Middle Kingdom picture is one of:

Archetypal (Three Yi)	**Ceremonial (Three Li)**
1 Inspirational principles	
	2 Principles of propriety
3 Pneumal channelling	
	4 Somatic constitution
5 Logic of interchange	
	6 Rules of conformity

The holy and the sacred are seen to form a ladder in soul between immortality and mortality but in a retrospective sense in which the veneration of ancestry plays a key civilizing part. The textual anthology which embodies connective process is best summarized by way of a spatial scheme:

The Book of Changes — The Book of Rites
The Spring: Autumn Annals of Lu
The Book of History — The Book of Poetry

The Ideographic Approach

This scheme emulates the Sages' Rule of Huang Di and carries the design of scriptural companionship into an interpretational situation for dedicants. Functionally speaking, though in a different direction, the texts of Middle Kingdom are a counterpart of the Hebrew texts of The Law and The Kingdom. Furthermore there is clear correlation between the characters of the chief figures in both traditions in the depiction of Divine relationship with the soul.
The Book of History lays down that The Path (to the center of Divine co-presence) must follow the unchanging Rule and Lesson of God.

Number, Time, Place and Cycle

The basic percept that Humanity depends for recognition of Divine relationship upon Heaven and Earth seems to have held good at all levels. Wisdom descended like a river out of Heaven and understanding flowed in response but like a river across the expanse of Earth. Accordingly the scriptures came into being to suit inner recognition according to the level of explanation. The media of companionship emerged as:

1. Divine Covenant, Myth and Legend, Inner: Outer Dialogue.
2. Next came history, poetry, cyclicity, Divine Oracle and Divine Ordinance.
3. Finally came the relating of these to external reception.

At level 1 the spatial discipline of digital number, as applied in ascent according to the Dragon Map, was associated with the idea of a heavenly river, called *He* (see Appendix B).

Key to the Dragon Map

	7-2	
8-3	10–5	9-4
	8-3	

Its spatial reception was as the Tortoise Writing, associated with the idea of an earthly river called Luo.

Key to the Tortoise Writing

4	9	2
3	5	7
8	1	6

Myth and legend were connected with cyclical descent according to a set of Cyclic Signs. Finally heavenly and earthly maps were made to explain the relationship between soul and body.

At level 2 the logic of interconnection in meaning was provided by the Sexagenary Cycle, in which twelve 'heavenly stems' were set against ten 'earthly branches'. The Spring:

Autumn Annals reflects this culturally and within the dimensions of history and poetry on one side and mind and nature on the other.

In the context of living the inner life of dedication the gist of all these insights amounted to reciprocity and interaction between Doctrine of The Mean and Path of Righteousness.

Inevitably some of the insights found their way outwards into the regulation and mores of the civilization.

Rationale of Scriptural Companionship

This reconstruction begins with the statement in *jin fu jing* that there are Five Robbers in the mind, emanating from Heaven. In the literature of The Sages these are amplified as five pneumal agents or entities called *gui shen*. These can best be seen in the following relative scheme:

Pneumal Entities (Gui Shen)

Ju Shou
in Contemplation (Metal)

Xuan Ming
in Conscience (Water)

Hou Tu
in Actuality (Earth)

Ju Meng
in Intuition (Wood)

Ju Yong
in Perception (Fire)

Their operation was seen as a rota:

Order	Symbolic Element	Mode
4	Wood	Intuition
5	Fire	Perception
1	Earth (soil)	Actuality
2	Metal	Contemplation
3	Water	Conscience

The governing principle was that any one is framed by the other four.

This symbolism of inner functioning, which links via the number 5 with the Dragon Map and Tortoise Writing of Huang Di, was outwardly complemented by observation of the universe and creation.

The night sky was seen as dividing into four quadrants around the Pole Star. Each quadrant received the name of an animal characteristic of each of the four seasons:

	North / Winter BLACK WARRIOR	
East / Spring AZURE DRAGON	*Centre* Pole Star	West / Autumn WHITE TIGER
	South / Summer VERMILION BIRD	

Accordingly an equation could be struck between cardinal points of direction and the phases of seasonal cycle. From this climate could be used as an analogy for human feelings (to be transcended in the life of dedication).

Finally, an explanation is given in the *shu jing* (Book of History) of The Great Plan of God. Summarized this appears as:

Function	System	Idiomatic presentation
1 Attention	5 Elements	Water, Fire, Metal, Wood, Earth
2 Recollectedness	5 Reverences in affairs	Demeanour, Speech, Sight, Hearing, Thought (with inner and outer effects)
3 Government	8 Productions	Husbandry, Exchange, Sacrifices, Works, Instruction, Crime, Hospitality, Army
4 Timing	5 Regulators	Threefold arrangement (see note 1)
5 Centrality	Excellence (Huang Ji)	Diffuses blessing through Son of Heaven to People, who yield loyalty. Centre of discrimination
6 Self-Regulation	3 Attributes of equalisation	Heavenly, Human Earthly (see note 2)

Part I The Family of The Way and The Grace of God

7 Self-examination	7 Doubts 6 Resolutions	Characteristic cultural metaphors, prognostic of weather and milfoil
8 Verification	6 Degrees 5 Alternatives	Climatic metaphors Seasonable – good Persistent – bad
9 Circumstance	5 Blessings	Life, wealth, health, morality, purpose
	6 Extremities	Misfortune, sickness, sorrow, poor resource, wickedness, weakness

Note 1: External Correlates

Regulator	**Examiner**	**Product**
Solar year	Sovereign	Rhythm
Month	Nobility	Tidal intensity
Day	Subordinates	Light, warmth
Planets	Sun	Registration
Intercalation	Mysterious	Solar, lunar and seasonable timings

Note 2: Correspondence

Heavenly	**Human**	**Earthly**
Correctness, directness in peace and tranquility	Strength of Government in violence and disorder	Mildness of Government in harmony and order

Mastery and Discipleship

The third and outermost tier of texts in the ideographic tradition of dedication to The Way and The Grace of God reflects experience of pneumal and somatic streaming. The four great texts can not only be seen to form one anthology but study of their content through indexing verifies their common ground. Nevertheless to the outside world they represented two different religious processes and, because Filial Son of dedication had not received personal identity, the religion of The Lord Buddha also came to be accepted in China. That illustrates the difference between the dedication of life to internal relationship and its separation from the way of the ordinary external world.

The teaching anthology can be appreciated as a quaternity of companionship having the following scheme:

Pneumal Stream	**Somatic Stream**
Inner	***Earlier***
The *Dao De Jing* of Lao Zi	The Analects (*Lun Yu*) of Confucius
Outer	***Later***
The Writings of Zhuang Zi (Zhuang Zi Shu)	The Mencius (Meng Ke)

The two pneumal texts are ascribed to masters but the two somatic texts to the disciples of masters. However the quaternity centers upon orthodoxy of dedication.

Since it becomes apparent that, during mortality, the pneuma conditions the active approach and the soma the passive, the anthology can be seen in the following terms:

The Active Way	*The Passive Way*
The Way of Loving Discovery	The Way of Sublime Quality
The Character of Partnership	The Nature of Relationship

Now the textual companionship appears through:

Elegy	Discursion
Prose	Teaching

These forms were lent to:

THE WAY OF LOVING DISCOVERY
(*Lun Yu*, Analects of Confucius)

I ETHICS OF ATTENTION

1 The Root of Loving Will
2 Divinity in Government
3 The Li and Musicality
4 Practice of Loving Will
5 Balancing Conduct and Words
6 Recollectedness and Overcoming
7 Models of Intention
8 Maintenance of Standards
9 Maintenance of Balance
10 Maintenance of Equability

II ETHICS OF PRACTICE

11 Treading after Goodness
12 Divinity and Merit
13 Fitness for Responsibility
14 Accomplishment and Completion
15 Holding to The Golden Rule
16 Family Economy
17 Sheer Good Taste
18 Apposite Humility
19 Door of Reality
20 Natural Purity and Middle Way

THE CHARACTER OF PARTNERSHIP
(*Meng Ke*, The Mencius)

I The Source of Love and Strength
II Accordance with Divinity
III The Foundation of Greatness
IV Balance and Happiness
VI The Way of Truth
VII Entering Service

THE WAY OF SUBLIME QUALITY
(*Dao De Jing* of Lao Zi)

Ennead One — The Scene of Partnership
Ennead Two — Exploration of Content
Ennead Three — Becoming someone
Ennead Four — Channelling Love
Ennead Five — Complying with The Law
Ennead Six — Spontaneous Morality
Ennead Seven — Learning About Salvation
Ennead Eight — Real Compassion
Ennead Nine — Steering The Course of Love

THE NATURE OF RELATIONSHIP
(*Zhuang Zi Shu*, The Writings of Zhuang Zi)

I Understanding Imagination
II Understanding Unity of Existence
III Understanding Non-existence

Chapter Five

The Alphabetical Approach

The Chinese branch of the family of scriptures of The Way and The Grace of God has been shown to reconstitute itself as a structured library. For Divine authority the texts look back at central authority, originating before Earliest Antiquity. Their librarial structure is equally the structure of the scriptural companionship with its dedicant readers. Not only does a process of discovery of Divine relationship unfold but Humanity, which appears in relation to Heaven and Earth, has a self in which reside both Superior Man and Petty Man. The narrative setting for scriptural expansion is of the building of Middle Kingdom amidst outer States, all within Divine Empire surrounded by Wild Tribes. There is mention, in the dao de jing, of The Law as being 'what it is' (i.e. above commentary).

Although the material for the first part of Genesis in the Bible is now thought to have emanated from the Sumerian culture in Mesopotamia, which used cuneiform script, the Bible as an entity has always been an ascent through several alphabetical languages. Since spelled words do not have a pictorial element in parallel with a homophonic context the methodology of scriptural composition must be less direct than in ancient China. Nevertheless the Bible as a library, now constituting *The Holy Bible*, manifests a structure formed by cumulative anthological building and having both sequence and symmetry of companionship with its reader. The immediate difference is that whereas the Chinese scriptures are analytical in type those of the Bible are devotional. Moreover, whilst early Genesis is retrospective of The Creation, there is forward prospection from the Patriarchs.

Whilst the adoption of compositional methodology similar to that of ideographic scripture can only be assumed, pending full academic research on such lines, there are sufficient and strong similarities of various kinds to warrant examination of how *The Holy Bible* accompanies the reader and of what this companionship discloses about the Divine relationship with the individual.

Chapter Six

Points of Similarity

The two great similarities between the ideographic and the alphabetical texts are, of course, dedication to The mysterious Way and The manifest Grace of God and the absolute recognitive terms of Heaven and Earth with which both Huang Di and Genesis begin. Next comes the figure of The Son, as the pivot of the life of dedication.

The Four Sages of China are:

1. King Tai Tan Fu (Fu Xi), who led the people to the holy mountain.

2. His grandson King Wen, who kept faith during a period of great tyranny.

3. The Duke of Zhou (Zhou Gong), who wrote the constitution for the realm of Middle Kingdom.

4. Confucius, who took the centrality of Middle Kingdom outwards into Lu State through both example and teaching.

These figures respectively resemble Moses, King David, King Solomon and the Old Testament Man of God.

The texts of *Dao* and of *De* contain the Three *Yi* and Three *Li*, which the teaching texts hold as ideal precepts of dedication. These correlate with, though transcended by, the Divine Oracles and Ordinances received by Moses on Mount Sinai. The *Yi* point towards solomonic wisdom and the *Li* towards davidic praise. In this connection it is noteworthy that the Chinese Odes are a kind of precursor to the Hebrew Psalms and that the Chinese Book of Musicality (see Appendix E) gives a unique rationale of inner musicality.

Finally, two apparently editorial insertions suggest awareness of a supracultural family of scriptural composition. In the Old Testament Moses found his vocation in Midian and married the daughter of a priest, Jethro, who subsequently advised him as to leadership before he came to Mount Sinai and the Divine giving of The Law. In the New Testament the story of Epiphany concerns three unnamed Kings of East. The Chinese Book of History begins with the stories of three founding *Di* (August Emperors): Yao, Shun and Yü.

Appendix A

Text of the Covenant in Secret (Yin Fu Jing)

(Tr. Beth McKillop)

I

1. When one contemplates The Way of Heaven, and observes the practices of Heaven, everything accomplishes itself.

2\. i. To Heaven belong the Five Robbers; and seeing this one apprehends how they prosper.

ii. The Five Robbers are present in the mind and when one can set them in action as in the manner of Heaven all space and time are in one's hands and all transformations are born in The Self.

3\. i. Heaven's nature is in Man.

ii. There is a spring (a power source) in the human heart.

iii. Humanity is determined by establishing The Way of Heaven.

4\. i. When Heaven exerts its power of slaying, the Shifting Stars have easy night lodging.

ii. When Earth exerts its power of slaying, Dragons and Serpents appear on dry land.

iii. When Humanity exerts its power of slaying, Heaven and Earth return and repeat.

iv. When Heaven and Earth exert in concert their power of slaying, the Myriad Mutations fix their base.

5. i. The nature is here clever and there stupid; and the one quality may lie concealed in the other.

ii. The abuse of The Nine Apertures takes place in the three most important, and these may be now in movement and now at rest.

iii. When Fire arises in Wood the trouble once begun is sure to destroy; when the villainy arises in The State it is certain that disintegration will follow.

iv. The One who cultivates his knowledge wisely is called The Sage.

II

6. i. It is the pattern of The Way for Heaven at one moment to give life and at another to take it away.

ii. Heaven and Earth steal from The Whole Creation; The Whole Creation steals from Humanity; Humanity steals from The Whole Creation.

iii. When The Three Thieves act, The Three Powers (which they embody) are at rest.

iv. Hence it is said: "During the time of nourishment all the members are properly ordered; when The Springs of Motion come into play all Transformations occur in peace".

7. i. Man knows that things are spiritual but he does not know the means whereby what is spiritual is so.

ii. Sun and Moon have their definite times and they are fixed in being great and small; the functions of intellect thereby take life; and spiritual illumination comes through this.

8. The motivating power of The Thieves cannot be seen and can not be known by anyone in The World. Having it, The Superior Man strengthens his body. Having it, The Petty Man makes light of The Divine Ordinances.

III

9. i. The blind hear well and the deaf see well.

ii. To exhaust the advantage from a single source is ten times better than using a multitude.

10.i. The heart is quickened by things from outside; yet meets death among things from outside.

ii. The Spring of Life is in the eyes.

iii. Heaven has no compassion but so it is that there is Great Compassion for both the clap of thunder and the gust of wind come without any plan.

11.i. Perfect joy is in the overflowing satisfaction of The Nature.

ii. Perfect tranquillity is in the purity of The Nature.

iii. When Heaven seems to be most self-centered its operation is at its most altruistic.

iv. As for The Animals one controls them through their very essence.

12.i. Life is the root of death and death the root of life.

ii. Compassion springs from injury and injury from compassion.

13.i. The Stupid Man through the patterns and laws of Heaven and Earth becomes sage; I through the patterns and laws of Seasons and Experience become wise.

ii. He in his stupidity is perplexed by sagacity; I in my freedom from stupidity am the same.

iii. He considers The Sage to be extraordinary; I do not consider my sagacity to be so.

iv. Therefore it is said: "He who sinks into Water or enters into Fire brings destruction upon himself."

14.i. The Way of Spontaneity is still; and so it is that Heaven and Earth and The Whole Creation have life.

ii. The Way of Heaven and Earth is gradual; and so it is that The Dark and The Light overcome each other.

iii. The Dark and The Light displace each other and The Changes and The Transformations proceed.

iv. Therefore The Sage knows that The Way of Spontaneity cannot be resisted and applies self-regulation.

15. The Way of Perfect Stillness cannot be elaborated by rules and calendars but it would seem that there is a wonderful Vessel out of which come the Ten Thousand Xiang, the Eight Trigrams and The Cycle of Sixty; the springs of The Spirit and of The Pneuma are hidden in it; the way in which The Dark and The Light displace each other (also); and all these come brightly forward into understanding.

Note: The term 'Ten Thousand' has the sense of myriad. Xiang means likenesses.

Appendix B

The Dragon Map and Tortoise Writing (see Chapter 3)

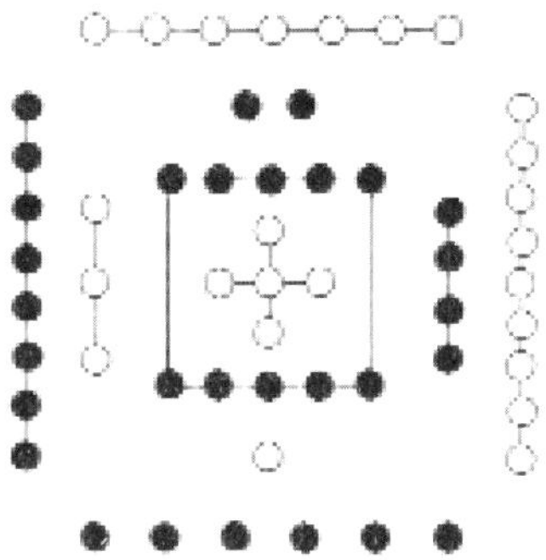

The Dragon Map
He T'u

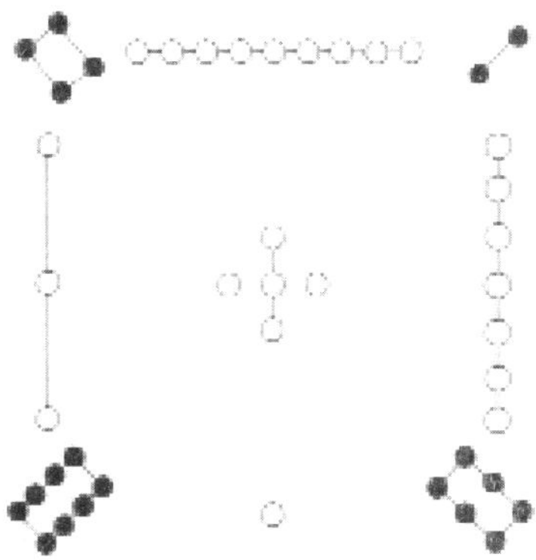

The Tortoise Writing
Luo Shu

Appendix C

Divided Synopsis of Annals of The Bamboo Books

THE MYTH

The Five Dominances descend out of centrality into sound association.

Dominance One: *Xian Yuan* Dynasty

Myth travels from Pole Star to settled Empire, from Vapors to Earthly Reign and from Mists to He Tu and Luo Shu. Earthquake precedes Imperial death. Idea enters dream. Rainbow becomes virtue. Rhythm evokes dance.

Dominance Two: *Tao and Tang* Dynasties

Centrality has Dragon of announcement and conception. Attention enters Modality of Timing and Succession. Revulsion enters Raising and Occupation. Regularity enters Sincerity through Musicality.

Dominance Three: *Xia He* Dynasty

Regulation of Flow produces The Great Plan. Nourishment enters life-span. Reign is followed by mourning. Escape enters Return. The De preserves Inheritance. Loss precedes Restoration. Fraternal relationship has Reward. Head of Family. Superstition enters Music of East. Alternation of Succession. Diversion precedes Displacement.

Dominance Four: *Shang/Yin* Dynasty

Relational Number enters 7,8,9 with name, expedition and interpretation. Ministry is rewarded. The cultivation of The *De* reveals extent of wickedness. Reverence enters possession of self. Mulberry Tree signifies attention to conduct. Resolute extinction of evil enters praise and revives ceremony. Familiarity breeds intolerance. Appreciation enters restraint. Tyranny leads to liberation.

Dominance Five: *Zhou* Dynasty

The sacred resists the birth of the new. By service Cultivation evokes response. Humility rises to distinction. Dreaming releases transforming influence. Integration brightens soul. Prayer is answered. Regency establishes Institutions and Music, Ritual Usage enters renewal. Exploratory effort captures new attitudes. Poor regulation and timing undermine and divide rulership. Sounds have similarity.

THE LEGEND

The Five Regimens descend from ideal life-span into standard measure.

Regimen One: Xian Yuan Dynasty

Huang Di lived 100 years and saw Cap with Pendants, Robes of Distinction and Colors of Clouds. He named his Officers Green, Vermilion, White and Black. (These correlate with Morning, Evening, Day, Night (cf. The Creation described in Genesis). Male and Female Tortoises arrived. Sacrifice began at the Luo. Barbarian tribes began to submit. The text mentions four successors and the titles four reigns with dynastic titles. Calendar cycle and Delineated alternation are founded in astronomy. Individual and State conflict begins.

Regimen Two: Tao and Tang Dynasties

The reign of Yao introduces observation, inheritance, inspection, division of Empire in 12 Provinces, pleasure, penal code, mission, cyclic sacrifice, principality, inspection and oversight of The People. The reign of Shun introduces restoration to 9 Provinces, Temple of Ancestry, Dance.

Regimen Three: Xia He Dynasty

Da Yu begins a period of 17 reigns. The capital city is the hub of Empire and moves West of the He. Music of East is made. The Hordes attack Empire. Inter-State war begins. Seasons are introduced in Regions and States, and Assembly of Princes begins. The Emperor's Tour of inspection begins and Princes attend Court to pay homage. The Hordes are recognized. Gui, the last Ruler, commences Periodicity of Cycle.

Regimen Four: Shang/Yin Dynasty

Counting Gui there are 10 Signs of Cyclicity of Rule named Gui, Bing, Ren, Jia, Ding, Geng, Ji, Mou, Yi, Xin. They permeate 30 Reigns. Deteriorating rulership is counteracted by improving ministerial capacity. Metal money is introduced. The Army is founded in West with power to deal with offense in State. The Duke of Zhou builds Imperial College and Spiritual Tower. King Wen hands over to King Wu.

Regimen Five: Zhou Dynasty

The fifth period has 34 reigns from Wu to Yin. The Way of Heaven is re-established with first fruits, measurement of ground, organized principality, imperial sacrifice. A regency re-introduces myth of institution. Azure Dragon and Black Warrior bring a figure and red characters, pre-figuring the Qin and Han dynasties. Institution and Constitution are set up. State Capitals are moved and come under threat. Inter-State relationships develop. The He is diverted into a marsh with outlet canals. Wells and dykes are developed. The Standard of Shadow Measure is lengthened and heightened.

Appendix D

Synopsis of The Divine Dialogue (*Su Wen*)

BOOK I

The Fall from Grace

1. Synchronicity, Age and The Right Way
2. The Foundation of Humanity
3. Breath of Heaven and Flavors of Earth
4. Evil Influence, Viscera, Mind and Spirit

BOOK II

The Foundation of Soul

5. Victory of Virtue over Disease
6. Binary Correspondence – Parting and Meeting
7. Trinary Correspondence – Variety, Spirituality and Virtue

BOOK III

Enumeration of The Good

8. Ingenuity and Subtlety
9. Complexity and Harmony
10. Visceral Connection
11. Nourishment and Treatment

BOOK IV

The Will to Healing

12. Treatment, Art and Unity
13. Reasons for Inner and Outer Division
14. Healing, Will and Immunity
15. Discrimination by Colors and Pulse
16. Rules and Regions of Morbidity

BOOK V

The Pulsating Organization

17. The Ingredients of Coalescence
18. Feeling and Pulsation

BOOK VI

Universe of Life and Death

19. Precious Mechanism
20. Health and Homeostasis

BOOK VII

The Modulation of Relationship

21. Systems and Viscera
22. Elements and Regulation
23. Comprehensive Modular Explanation
24. Examination, Location, Condition and Identification

Part I The Family of The Way and The Grace of God

BOOK VIII
The Creation for Service

25. Discovering The Middle Way
26. Caring for The Vessel of The Spirit
27. Overcoming Evil
28. The Laws of Mortality
29. Constancy and Osmosis
30. Freedom and Corruption

BOOK IX
Human Desire and Perfect Peace

31. Remnant and Survival
32. Influence, Cycle and Timing
33. The War between Force and Submission
34. The Way of Peace

Appendix E

Inner Musicality

The first biblical reference to musicality occurs in the family of Cain (*Genesis* 4:21). The gift was handed down to David (1 *Samuel* 16:16) and was the cause of his introduction to Saul. Music entered religious worship when King David rediscovered the Ark of The Covenant (2 *Samuel* 6:15). In 1 *Chronicles* 15 it is joined with words, in song. Music is linked with praise after the dedication of the national temple by King Solomon (2 *Chronicles* 7). Praise was re-instituted by King Hezekiah (2 *Chronicles* 29).

The only definitive text explaining musicality as natural integration of ascent towards God occurs in the scriptures of The Way and The Grace of God of ancient China. In the reconstituted library of *Dao* (Way) and *De* (Grace) and between the texts of Huang Di and the main teaching texts stand the Three *Yi* and Three *Li* ascribed to The Sages. Of these the *Li*, or ceremonials, survive as three stages. The third stage, the *Li Ji* or Book of Rites contains the *Yue Ji* (Record of Musicality) known secularly as the 'Book of Music' .

Summary of 'The Record of Musicality'

I Rest and Movement

Since (under The Ancient Kings) sorrow, joy, anger, reverence and love impress themselves upon sound there is interaction between words, airs and character. The *Li*, The *Yue*, Laws and Punishments are instituted to order the mind. The changes in interrespondence (between externals, mind, feelings, and voice modulation) can be symbolized in Music, Shields and Axes, Plumes and Oxtails (types of dance and pantomime). Only Superior Man can know inner music. His Five Notes signify Ruler, Ministers, People, Affairs and Things (i.e. ingredients of government) – either in harmony or ruination. Therefore a means towards self-realization exists.

At birth the human nature is still, but desire increases with knowledge. When it gets out of hand Humanity becomes what it beholds. The Li and The Yue are intended to return feelings to normality. Inner music produces stillness. Outer ceremony produces elegance. Reciprocity is therefore distinguishable in ease and facility.

The constants in the harmony and distinction of Heaven and Earth are respect, love, time and merit. Instrumentation and accompaniment of the Li and the Yue echo these and enable interaction to be practised. Instrumentation, praise, service and sacrifice come naturally to The People.

Only The Sage can make perfect music, for it decays with The Fall. The *Li* and the *Yue* resemble righteousness and benevolence because they embody normality and harmony, are framed by the variety of The Creation, and arise by accordance with production and change.

They represent due order between male and female life in distinction and interaction. The *Yue* appear in Grand Beginning and The *Li* in Completion of Place. Through their rest and movement come All Things between Heaven and Earth.

II The Role of Musicality

Music originates, in Antiquity, in the making and use of the Five-stringed Lute of *Shun Di* and the expression of royal approval by Feudal Lords through Gui's compositions. Son of Heaven uses music and pantomime to indicate reward and service. The Five dynastic musics express brilliance, completeness, continuity, greatness and quality.

Illness, famine and failure arise in Humanity from unseasonable interaction between Heaven and Earth. The Ancient Kings instruct in it because it influences Humanity and changes manners and customs. Grief, pleasure, joy and anger are manifest in mental faculty, although they have no rules and move according to external causes. The Five Notes declare six interactive levels between Ruler and People.

In mind, founded in feelings and nature, there are four phases:

i. Measure - which adapts to meaning

ii. Life-force - which expresses modality of moral worth

iii. The Yang/Yin indication

iv. Strong/Weak interphasing.

These are succeeded by schools and by grades of increase, representation and manifestation.

Fall into disorder is despised by Superior Man because cause and effect correspond. Things affect each other according to class. In Humanity a note has response from a spirit, whether evil or good. Hence Superior Man returns to the correct course and The De is manifest in note and tone, Accompaniment by lutes, movements with shields and axes, arrangements of plumes and oxtails, pipes and flutes. Details, between Heaven and Earth, correspond in the Notes, the

Colors, the Eight Winds and Musical Accords, the Composition. In the full course of music there is repose All Beneath Heaven. Ears and eyes, blood and energy, influence and manners are defined. Because desire comes under regulation where there is music there is joy.

Superior Man uses music to harmonize will and affections. The De, music and accompaniment actualize energy and harmony. Pantomime discharges desire. Music displays The De. Ceremony returns feeling and carries mind to origination. Feudal Lords bestow gifts.

III The Role of Liturgy

Theory, of the *Yue* and the *Li*, embraces the whole nature of Humanity by representing sharing and difference. They impart embodiment to the subtle and material and regulate father/son, ruler/subject duties.

Power of musicality enables Great Man to make Heaven and Earth respond. But, in this, practice of attributes is above practice of art. Completion precedes action.

Music and sound are not the same, for The Fall occurs through antecedence, The Sages, airs of The *De* and airs of Change.

There are unison, instrumentation, discrimination and association of ideas. The music of King *Wu* represents time of engagement. It symbolizes representation of fact, attitude, enthusiasm and government as personified by King *Wu*, *Tai Gong*, and in the *Zhou* and *Shao* realms. There is re-enactment of victory over evil, deliverance of The People and abolition of weapons of war. Five great things – archery, uniformity, sacrifice, audience and husbandry – are substituted. There is penetration by the ways of *Zhou* and interaction of *Li* and *Yue*.

Superior Man teaches that, in mastering the *Yue*, one regulates mind and heart. In mastering The *Li* one obtains gravitas and respect. Perfect harmony and perfect observance are the inside and outside of Humanity. When both interact nothing beneath Heaven is difficult to manage. There must be response and introspection, and from them arise pleasure and repose.

The changes, required by the nature, are modulations and movements. The Ancient Kings frame music to represent the changes in joy and anger.

The Odes divide The *De* into five modulations. Therefore to set the self right and display The *De* one can select from the *Da Ya*, *Xiao Y*a, *Shang* and *Qi* (dynastic odes), according to need. The *Ya* emanate from Kingdom. The *Shang* and *Qi* emanate from The Five *Di* and Three Dynasties, and confer decision and deference with courage and righteousness.

Singing, utterance and expression are succeeded by movement of the members.

Appendix F

List of Translations of the Ideographic Scriptures

The texts mentioned in this survey are to be found within the following selections, available in central libraries if not in print.

Largest Selection

1. *The Sacred Books of China*, Tr. James Legge. Published as part of 'The Sacred Books of The East' (Müller Edn.). Oxford University Press 1891 and later. Currently in print through Hong Kong University, Dover Publications Inc. New York (most), and Motilal Banarsidass, Delhi.

The *Huang Di* Anthology

1. *Yin Fu Jing*, within 'The Texts of Taoism' (see 1 above).
2. *Annals of The Bamboo Books*, within the Shu Jing (see 1 above).
3. *The Yellow Emperor's Classic of Internal Medicine*, Tr. Ilza Veith. University of California Press. 1972.

The *Yi* and The *Li*

1. *The Text of Yi King*, Z.D. Sung, 1934 (The Shanghai Press)
2. *The I Ching or Book of Changes*, Richard Wilhelm, English retr. from the German by Cary F. Baynes. (Routledge & Kegan Paul).

3. *I Ching. The Book of Changes*, John Blofeld. (Mandala Books).
4. *The Classic of Changes: A New Translation of I Ching as interpret ed by Wang Bi*, Richard John Lynn, Columbia University Press, 1994.
5. *The I Li*, translated by John Steele, (Swatow 1913), pub. London (in British Library).
6. *The Zhou Li*, French tr. only) Le Tcheou-Li ou Rites des Tcheou, Feu Edouard Biot, (L'Imprimerie National), 1851 (Paris), (reprint available Taiwan).
7. *The Ceremonial Usages of The Chinese BC 1121, or Chow Le Kwan Choo*, Tr. W.R.Gingell 1852.
8. *The Li Ji,* (see 1 above).

Translations of the *Dao De Jing*

1. *Speculations,* Chalmers, J. 1868 (London).
2. *The Texts of Taoism,* Legge, J. 1891, 1927 (Müller edn) OUP (London).
3. *Lao-Tze's Tao-teh-kin,* Carus, P. (Open Court Pub.Co.) 1898 (Chicago).
4. *The Taoteh King,* Kingsmill, T.W. 1899 (Shanghai).
5. *The Canon of Reasons and Virtue,* Carus P., P.1903, 1913 (Chicago).
6. *The Light of China,* Heysinger I.W. 1903 (Chicago).
7. *The Tao-Teh King,* Parker E.H. (n.d.).
8. *Tao Teh Chin,* Lo Ka Ping. 1903 (Hong Kong).
9. *Tao Teh Ch'ing Old*, W.G., Daniel 1904 (London).
10. *The Book of The Simple Way of Laotze,* Old, W.G., (Wellby, P.), 1904, 1943 (London).

12. *The Tao Teh King*, Medhurst C.S. 1905, 1972 (Chicago).
13. *Tao-Te-King*, Mears, I. 1916 (Glasgow).
14. *The Sayings of Lao Tzu Giles*, L. 1922 (London).
15. *The Way and Its Power,* Waley, A. (George Allen, Unwin) 1934, 1977 (London).
16. *Tao Te Ching*, Bhikshu Wai-Tao and Goddard D. 1935 (Santa Barbara).
17. *The Lao-tzu*, Hu Tse-ling, (Canadian Mission Press) 1936 (Chengtu).
18. *Tao Te Ching*, Ch'u Ta-kao Unwin 1937, 1972 (London).
19. *The Way of Life*, Bynner W., (John Day) 1944, 1946, 1972 (New York).
20. *The Way of Acceptance*, Ould, H., (Dakers) 1946 (London).
21. *The Wisdom of Laotse*, Lin Yutang, (Joseph, M.) 1948, 1958 (London), (Manners D. and Ault M) 1948 (Meopham Green).
22. *Truth and Nature*, Chenghiu, (World Book Co). 1949
24. *The Great Sinderesis*, Poyton,O., (Hassell Press) 1949 (Adelaide).
25. *Tao Te Ching*, Duyvendak J.J.L. (John Murray) 1954 (London).
26. *The Way of Life*, Blakney, R.B. 1955,1957,1964 (New York).
27. *The Lao Tzu*, Hsu Chao 1961 (Taipeh).
28. *Tao Te Ching Wu*, J.C.H., (Sih, P.K.T.ed) (St. Johns UP) 1961 (New York).
29. *Tao Te Ching,* Lau, D.C. 1963 (Penguin).
30. *Tao Te Ching*, Mackintosh C.A., (Wheaton) 1971(London). ditto 1982 (Hong Kong).
31. *Tao Te Ching*, Gia-Fu Feng and Jane English: Wildwood House 1973 (London).
32. *Lao Tzu*, Ch'en Ku-ying (tr. Young & Ames) 1977 (San Francisco).

33. *The Way of The Ways*, Schocken, M.H. 1982 (New York).
34. *Wisdom of the Daoist Masters*, Wieger, L. (tr. Bryce, D.) 1984 (Llanerch).
35. *The Tao of Leadership*, Heider, J. (Adapt.) 1985 (Atlanta).
36. *Lao-tze, the Great Thinker*, Alexander, G.G. 1985 (London).

Translations of *Analects of Confucius (Lun Yu)*

1. *Confucian Analects*, Legge J. 1861 & 1893 (Hong Kong and London)
2. *The Lun Yu*, Wade, Sir Thomas. 1864 & 1869
3. *The Chinese Classics Part I,* Legge. J., 1887 (New York.)
4. *The Confucian Analects,* Jennings W., 1895 (London & New York)
5. *The Discourse and Sayings of Confucius*, Ku Hung Ming, 1898 (Shanghai).
6. *Selected Sayings of K'ung the Master,* (greater part only). Upward. A., 1904 (London).
7. *The Sayings of Confucius*, Giles, L., (John Murray) 1907 (London).
8. *The Sayings of Confucius*, Lyall, L.A., (Longmans Green), 1909, 1925, 1935 (London).
9. *The Analects of Confucius,* Soothill W.E., 1910 (Yokohama).
10. *The Ethics of Confucius*, Dawson N.M. (Arr.). 1915 (New York and London).
11. *The Analects of the Conversation of Confucius with his disciples and certain others*, Soothill, W.E., (OUP) 1937 (London).
12. *The Wisdom of Confucius*, Lin Yu-t'ang, 1938 (New York).
13. *The Analects of Confucius*. Waley, A., (Allen & Unwin) 1949 (London).

14. *K'ung tzu chia yu*, Kramers, R.P., (E.J.Brill) 1950 (Leiden).
15. *The Sayings of Confucius*, Ware J.R., (Mentor Books) 1955 (New York). 1964 ditto (New American Library).
17. *Confucian Analects*, Pound, Ezra. (Peter Owen) 1956 & 1970 (London).
18. *Confucius, The Analects*, Lau D.C., (Penguin) 1979 (London).
19. *Confucius, The Analects*, Saur K.G. (Clive Bingley) 1980 (London).

Translations of *The Writings of Zhuang Zi*

1. *The Divine Classic of Nan Hua, being the works of Chuang Tsze,* (tr. into English). Balfour F.H. (Kelly & Walsh) 1881 (Shanghai).
2. *Chuang Tzu, Mystic, Moralist and Social Reformer*, Giles H.A.T., 1889 (Bernard Quaritch) (London). 1926 & 1961 (Allen and Unwin).
3. *The Texts of Taoism,* Legge J. (Müller edn) (Clarendon Press) 1891 & 1927 (London).
4. *Chuang Tzu. A new selected translation,* Yu-lan Fung (Commercial Press) 1931 (Shanghai).
5. *The Sayings of Chuang Chou*, Ware, J.R. (New American Library) 1963 (New York).
6. *Chuang Tzu. Basic Writings,* Burton Watson (Columbia UP) 1964 (New York and London).
7. *The Complete Works of Chuang Tzu*, 1968 (as above).
8. *The Way of Chuang Tzu,* Merton, Thomas . (New Directions) 1965 & 1969 (NewYork). 1970 (Allen and Unwin) London.
9. *Chuang Tzu. (Inner Chapters),* Gia-fu Feng and Jane English. (Wildwood House) 1974 London.

Appendix F

Translations of *The Mencius*

1. *The Works of Mencius,* Legge, J. 1861 (Hong Kong) 1894 (Oxford), (Edn. Müller) 1970 (New York)
2. *The Mind of Mencius,* Hutchinson, Rev. A.B., (Trubners Oriental Series) 1882
3. *Mencius*, Lyall, L.A., Longmans Green) 1932 (London)
4. *The Book of Mencius*, Giles L., (John Murray) 1942 (London)
5. *The Sayings of Mencius*, Ware J.R., (New York) (New American Library)1960
6. *Mencius,* Dobson, W.H.C.H., 1963 (Thompson) 1967 (OUP) (UNESCO)
7. *Mencius*, Lau D.C., (Harmonsworth Penguin)1970

PART II

The Written Companionship of *The Holy Bible*

6 THE REVELATION

The Book of Revelation

5 THE CHURCH

The Pauline Letters The General Letters
Timothy, Titus, Philemon
Acts of The Apostles

4 GOSPEL

Mark John
Matthew Luke

3 PROPHECY

Zechariah Malachi
Zephaniah Haggai
Nahum Habakkuk
Jonah Micah
Amos Obadiah
Hosea Joel
Ezekiel Daniel
Isaiah Jeremiah with
Lamentations

The Symmetry of *The Holy Bible*

2 KINGDOM

Ecclesiastes Song of Solomon

Psalms Proverbs

Esther Job

Ezra Nehemiah

Kings Chronicles

Ruth Samuel

Joshua Judges

1 THE LAW

Numbers Deuteronomy

Leviticus

Genesis Exodus

Anthologies

The Pentateuch 1

The Septuagint 3

The Vulgate 1-6

Chapter Seven

The Librarial Structure of *The Holy Bible*

From the reconstituted library of the texts of *Dao* and of *De* it can be seen that the Chinese branch of the family of dedication saw Divine relationship as a three-tier retrospection from life in the flesh to pure identity in God. From that standpoint it becomes practicable to look at scriptural developments in the western part of the family.

First, however, it is necessary to take an overall view of the anthological library as a structure against which to see the companionship it offers the reader and the understanding of relationship which that demonstrates. This is not readily apparent from only the sequential procession of texts but, when parallelism of nature and mind is taken into account, it follows smoothly.

The diagrammatic scheme on pages 62-3 may serve as a guide to the chapters which follow.

Chapter Eight

The Pentateuch

The name of the anthology, which is Greek, refers to five texts centered upon the ministry of Moses. Their arrangement centers, as befits the idea of a holy nation, upon *Leviticus*.

Genesis begins with an introduction to Divine relationship which, as in China, posits Heaven and Earth. Also, as in China, myth and legend combine. Eden, The Fall, The Flood and the Noahic Covenant follow (1-12).

Next comes a legend of transition in which Abram leaves Sumer for Egypt and then Canaan. He turns to God whilst Lot, his brother, turns to the world. Abram honored the Divine Covenant and entered renewal of self, marked by renaming as Abraham. There follow stories of the Hebrew Patriarchs Isaac, Jacob and Joseph which descend in turn through a view of the self in Divine relationship until they reach the world into which Moses was born.

The story of Moses begins in an alien country in which the people descended from the Patriarchs are enslaved. Moses, given royal upbringing, stands apart from establishment. He is forced to escape and finds his way into Midian, where he marries into the family of Jethro, a priest of unspecified denomination but manifestly of the tradition of The Way and The Grace of God. Moses receives his vocation and returns to liberate his people (*Exodus* 5-12).

Now begins the story of the coalescence of the people into a theocentric nation in the course of a journey into the unknown and of facing hardship (*Exodus* 13-17). Moses begins to feel the strain of leadership, and of intermediation between his people and God, but is joined by Jethro, who advises decentralization and delegation of authority (*Exodus* 18).

It is not long before Moses is drawn to the holy mountain of dedication (*Exodus* 19) where he receives The Divine Law and Commandments, together with The Covenant to be enshrined at the center of the holy nation and The Divine constitution and institutions.

Finally (*Exodus* 33) the nation is enabled to follow The Lord's guidance towards its promised land of settlement.

Leviticus, a latinized English title referring to consecration of life, sets out the nation's sacred institutions and rules for holy living.

Numbers, a title which refers to the counting of the nation before and after its journeying period, is a record of how it passed through privation and uncertainty and became organised as an army of God. The holy nation is prepared for the crossing of the Jordan river.

Deuteronomy, a word referring to its review of The Law, is also the last will and testament of Moses to the nation, and ends with his death and obituary. It is also an inner constitution for the twelve tribes in their entity as a holy nation.

Chapter Nine

The Septuagint – The Kingdom

Whilst the Septuagint anthology embodies the Pentateuch its additional range can be described as bounded at beginning and end by the Jordan river, now editorially made a figure for an integrative frontier for renewal in dedication to The Way and The Grace of God. The central turning point of the Septuagint is the vocation and ministry of Elijah.

The anthology divides into the texts of The Kingdom (*Joshua* to *Song of Solomon*) and the texts of Prophecy (*Isaiah* to *Malachi*). Both divisions can be seen as a series of steps made by parallel texts, there being seven in The Kingdom and eight in Prophecy.

In The Kingdom anthology the temple upon the holy mountain of Sion, within the nation's capital city, becomes the place of meeting where The King represents the nation before The Lord, The Son of Man (for Whom the Greek term was *Christos*). The course of the anthology can be traced as follows:

1. *Joshua and Judges*

Following the death of Moses, Joshua and Caleb lead the nation across the Jordan, though a part decides to settle on the near side after helping with the conquest of the Promised Land. The Ark of The Covenant is present during the gaining of a bridgehead. Canaan is taken and settled and Joshua renews The Covenant. After his death the nation is governed by a series of judges. In the absence of a Divinely appointed leader there arises serious dispute, some civil war and a general loss of sense of cohesion.

2. *Ruth and Samuel*

Ruth is an allegory of affinity. The Moabite widow of an expatriate Hebrew accompanies her mother-in-law back to Bethlehem, where she is guided to throw herself on the mercy of Boaz, a kinsman by marriage. In the end they are married, whereby the hereditary line continued which was to arrive at David.

Samuel, a text divided for the Septuagint into two halves, deals with the foundation of The Kingdom. The boy Samuel had been 'lent back' to The Lord by his mother in the custody of Eli, an old priest who maintained the temple at Shiloh. In due course Samuel received Divine vocation to judge the nation. He was to anoint its first king according to popular vote but Saul's reign failed and David was chosen in his place by The Lord. There ensues a time of oppression and conflict until the death of Saul. David then unites the nation and founds the theocratic Kingdom around the citadel of Sion in Jerusalem.

3. *Kings and Chronicles*

Both these texts were divided by the Septuagint editorship so that they form, in effect, an account of the Kingdom from four standpoints.

> 1 *Kings* covers the regression from the Davidic reign through the period of division into the kingdoms Israel and Judah.
> 2 *Kings* contains on the story of Elijah's ministry, the Babylonian captivity and the eventual release of Israel's king from imprisonment.
> 1 *Chronicles* is mainly about the kingdom of Judah under David and Solomon, including the design for the temple.
> 2 *Chronicles* cover's Solomon's implementation of David's charge to build and dedicate the temple. It tells of the Babylonian desecration of Jerusalem and the captivity of Judah, until Cyrus of Persia was moved to permit the temple's restoration.

The texts are detailed as regards the inner significance and outer symbolism of the temple and provide an historical background to the development of prophecy.

4. *Ezra and Nehemiah*

The first text describes the rebuilding of the temple and the second the rebuilding of the city wall, a symbolic pairing of actions to prepare for the nation's reconstitution.

5. *Esther and Job*

With these texts the fifth step of The Kingdom pairs sensibility and faculty of Divine relationship.

Esther, a beautiful Jewess who becomes the queen of Persia, is instrumental in the relief from oppression of her own people. It is a story of concern for others.

Job is, in effect, a drama about human fallibility which contains an intellectual debate about the place of suffering in the Divine relationship. Job is rebuked for presumption, becomes contrite and prospers.

6. *Psalms and Proverbs*.

At this, the sixth step, the companionship by scripture demonstrates praise in ascent from nature and wisdom in descent through mind. Here is shown reciprocity and interaction within the soul. The psalms arise out of nature and are accompanied by music. The proverbs are shown as coming from above into mind.

Both texts are in five parts. The arrangements can be described from their content as follows:

The Book of Psalms

1-41	The meaning of fellowship
42-72	The role of The King
73-89	Central intercession
90-106	Discovering God through praise
107-150	Fulness of life in God

The Book of Proverbs

Ch. 1-9	Wisdom from above
Ch. 10-24	The Path of Righteousness
Ch. 25-29	True knowledge and understanding
Ch. 30	The place of mystery in self-control
Ch. 31	The place of holy fear in virtue

7. *Ecclesiastes* and *Song of Solomon*

The final pairing in The Kingdom anthology is of inspiration with adoration.

In *Ecclesiastes* the Preacher is Solomon. He muses inwardly about all that happens in the world, ponders its meaning in the light of the certainty of physical death, and ends with superb poetry about the return of bodily elements to their original earth whilst the human spirit returns to God, its Giver.

In *Song of Solomon* the king utters a distillation of the 'one thousand and five songs' ascribed to him (1 *Kings* 4:32). The song of songs is a duet of love in an atmosphere of continuing wonder and longing.

Summary

That the companionship of the anthology of The Kingdom is with an ascent in devotion in the soul is without doubt.

Chapter Ten

The Septuagint – Prophecy

The story of Elijah is contained in 1 *Kings* 17-21 and 2 *Kings* 1,2. Elijah's ministry occurred in Israel during the reign of Ahab, a king who had married the Sidonian Jezebel who encouraged the worship of Baal.

First Elijah was called by The Lord into a desert. Then he was sent to lodge with a widow. There being a drought The Lord provided meal and oil. Elijah prayed that the widow's sick child be restored and this was granted. Then he was sent to tell Ahab to gather all the prophets of Baal at Mount Carmel.

There was a trial by Divine miracle (1 *Kings* 18) after which the prophets of Baal were slain. Ahab acknowledged The Lord's victory but Jezebel threatened Elijah, who fled into the wilderness. There The Lord gave him the command to anoint firstly a King for Syria then another for Israel, and Elisha as his own successor.

Finally, at the Jordan river, Elijah was taken up by a whirlwind into the heaven, leaving Elisha to continue the ministry in the earth.

The texts of prophecy, counting the two by Jeremiah as one, form eight steps in completion of Old Testament.

Isaiah and *Jeremiah*

These two great works begin a phase of scriptural companionship of a new order.

Isaiah looks forward to the eventual redemption of Israel and the Divine creation of new heavens and new earth.

Jeremiah's ministry was to sustain the remnant of the faithful so that there could be a return to God. He prophesied the redemption of Judah through Christ as King.

Ezekiel and *Daniel*

Both prophets were exiles, though at different times, and both had inner visions of Divine relationship in eternity. Ezekiel prophesied an everlasting Covenant and Daniel looked towards resurrection.

Hosea and *Joel*

The theme of *Hosea* is that since Divine love is greater than human offense, the return to God is all important. That of *Joel* is of Divine judgment and of the meaning of Sion.

Amos and *Obadiah*

Amos prophesies the purgation of sin and the ultimate

restoration of The Kingdom. *Obadiah* looks beyond worldly evil towards deliverance upon Mount Sion.

Jonah and *Micah*

Jonah is a highly allegorical text in which The Word of The Lord is shown to take priority over any human attitude. *Micah's* theme is of Divine mercy and constancy.

Nahum and *Habakkuk*

In *Nahum* there is insight that the Gospel lies ahead. Meanwhile, citing the case of Nineveh (see *Jonah*) the reality is that as one sows so shall one eventually reap. Habakkuk's prophecy is of unqualified joy and strength in God.

Zephaniah and *Haggai*

Zephaniah's message uses the symbolism of The Day of The Lord to confirm the Divine destiny of the holy nation. *Haggai* prophesies that work of rebuilding has ultimate Divine significance.

Zechariah and *Malachi*

The final two books foreshadow New Testament. *Zechariah* prophesies of Christ The Shepherd and of new Jerusalem. *Malachi*, an unattributed text, prophesies of The Messenger of The Lord, who would prepare His Way before Him.

Chapter Eleven

Gospel

By 'gospel' is meant the Good News of the life, ministry and Passion of Christ. There are four Evangels or witnesses.

As a scheme of quaternity the texts can be seen in the relative positions:

Mark	John
Matthew	Luke

Their standpoints of companionship are:

Plain Truth	The Word
Fulfillment of precedent	Eye-witness

Chapter Twelve

The Church

The penultimate stage of the biblical companionship begins with the baptism of the apostles with The Holy Spirit and the conferral on them of the power to witness to Christ.

The natural tendency in the world is to think of The Church as the organization of one religion amongst others. Yet what had happened was realization of the personal statement by Jesus: 'And I, if I be lifted up from the earth, will draw all men unto me'. (*John* 12:32). Christ had now to be known no longer as The Lord, The Son of Man' but as The Son of God and the Head of The Church.

The sub-anthology which now provides companionship can be seen in the three steps:

3. The Pauline Letters and the General Letters
2. *Timothy*, *Titus*, *Philemon*
1. *Acts of The Apostles*

Its scheme of the arrangement for companionship unfolds as:

3. Parallelism with active and passive streams of dedication of life.
2. Leadership of The Church in the world.
1. The basis of the new foundation

The detail of the third step can be expanded so as to appear as:

Pauline Letters	*General Letters*
Hebrews	Jude
Levantines	1-3 John
Grecians (I and 2 Cor)	I and 2 Peter
Romans	James

Chapter Thirteen

The Revelation

The final text stands alone and its reader is made privy to the revelation by Jesus to Saint John of the process arising out of The Holy Catholic and Apostolic Church.

This text too has the literary construction of four phases of process in dedication to The Way and The Grace of God.

Prophecy, particularly in the cases of *Ezekiel* and *Daniel*, had glimpsed potential. Therefore the reader has symbolic precedents for angelic and numinous symbolism, now to be extended.

The four literary phases are:

I (1-3) Seven works and their rewards.

II (4-10) The opening of a scroll of process with seven seals, by The Lamb of God before the company of Heaven.

III (11-18) Symbolism of process of truth.

IV (19-22) The Marriage of The Lamb with His Church, New Heaven and Earth and The City of God.

At the end of the revelation Christ gives the promise: 'Surely I come quickly.'

Epilogue

From the literary angle it appears that the major events in the production of the volume, *The Holy Bible*, were:

1. The consolidation into Greek of the Hebrew scriptures for the Alexandria Library, in the third century, called The Septuagint.
2. The consolidation into Greek of the Apostolic texts.
3. The production of the Latin peoples' Bible in the fourth century, called The Vulgate.
4. European retranslation resulting in The King James Version.
5. Twentieth century retranslations.

Again, from the literary angle, when emphasis is laid on companionship with the life of dedication to The Way and The Grace of God, the following ascending structural shape emerges:

7. The Revelation
6. The Church
5. Gospel
4. Prophecy
3. Hebrew texts of The Kingdom
2. Hebrew texts of The Law
1. The Chinese library.

Although, being scripture, all these anthologies stand above the literature of secular academe the anthology of Huang Di provides a rationale of linkage between soul and body, linkage increasingly accepted today as having physiological implications. There seems to be no logical reason why such continuity could not be put to connective use by conventional academic specializations.

Acknowledgments

Grateful thanks are due to the staff of the Department of Oriental Studies of the British Library.

Much use has been made of The New Scofield Reference Bible, Oxford University Press 1967 and of Bible Study software published by NavPress Software.

Publisher's Afternote

It will be proposed to publish certain preliminary studies to this book in an imprint to be called The Lectio Press. The imprint will also consider works from all academic disciplines which explore specialist implications of the ideas in this book.

First published in Great Britain by
THE LECTIO PRESS
in association with
ASHGROVE PUBLISHING
an imprint of Hollydata Publishers Ltd
55 Richmond Avenue
London N1 0LX

ISBN 1 85398 143 5

First Edition

Book design by Brad Thompson
Printed and bound in Malta by Interprint

"WE'RE MOVING"
ACTION-KIT

"WE'RE MOVING"
ACTION-KIT

The easy step-by-step guide to moving house

by Elizabeth and Ian Shaw

STAR

A Star Book
Published in 1990 by
W. H. Allen & Co. plc
Sekforde House
175/9 St John Street
London EC1V 4LL

Printed and bound in Great Britain by
Scotprint Ltd, Musselburgh, Scotland

ISBN 0 352 32442 2

Important

While the advice and information given is believed to be true and accurate at the time of going to press, neither the authors nor the publisher can accept any legal responsibility for any errors or omissions that may be made.

Introducing your "We're Moving!" Action-Kit

OK – so you're moving home! This is an exciting time for you, and probably a little worrying too. But take heart – you can make things go much more smoothly by making good use of your "We're Moving!" Action-Kit.

The kit does not deal with the legal and financial aspects of buying and selling property. Nor is it concerned with the purely personal questions which arise such as "Shall we take the carpets with us or not?" That's for you to decide.

What it does is to help you answer the questions: "Who needs to be told that I am changing my address? What do I have to tell them? How shall I tell them?"

Firstly, by making your way through the comprehensive **CHECKLIST**, you can quickly identify the various businesses, organisations, and people who should be included in your personal list of "who to tell". The Checklist is designed also to serve as a record of everything you do, making sure you don't overlook anything. It also leads you into the **GUIDE** which provides you with all sorts of information, comment, and advice on dealing with the more important services and facilities you use. These include rates, electricity, TV rental, insurances, and telephones, to name but a few.

The **LETTERS** provide you with a quick and efficient way of communicating the relevant details of your move to those organisations which provide you with goods, services, and facilities.

This Action-Kit is therefore a practical guide, with detailed and down-to-earth information and advice to help you when you are faced with telling people "We're Moving!"

The actual costs of certain services (for example, the redirection of mail by the Post Office) are quoted. We also refer to a number of current practices and regulations which may affect the home-mover (for example, those concerned with the issue of firearms certificates). We have to point out that, while we have made every effort to ensure that these details are accurate at the time of going to press, they are subject to amendment, sometimes at short notice, by the authorities and organisations concerned.

The advice given in the Guide is based on information obtained from the many organisations we have consulted, and we believe it to be sound and relevant. We cannot, however, accept responsibility for any inaccuracies which may result from changes in, or differences between, the policies and practices of similar organisations. If in doubt on any point, you are advised to make direct contact with the relevant organisation in order to obtain help with your particular problem.

We wish you GOOD LUCK! with your move.

Elizabeth and Ian Shaw

The Checklist

How to use the checklist

1 Read down the alphabetical list of "Things to check" and put ticks in the boxes alongside all those items that apply to you. For example, if you belong to the AA (item 1 on the list), put a tick in the first box in the column headed "Does this apply?" If not, leave the box blank and continue down the list.

2 When you have ticked all the relevant boxes, check the number in the column headed "Guide page no" against each item you have ticked, and refer to the relevant page in the Guide section for further information, comment, and advice.

3 Record in the "Notes/Action" column any particular action you need to take and the date by which you need to take it, or any problem you need to resolve (eg write, phone, or call; obtain new insurance quotations).

4 Look again at the boxes which you have ticked. An "L" alongside the box means that there is a special pre-printed letter in the Letters section which you can use to write to this particular organisation.

Note: the Letters section also includes a number of "open" letters which you can send to other organisations.

5 As you deal with each item in your list (eg when you post a letter), insert the date in the column headed "Date completed".

6 Keep a check on your progress by regularly looking down your list of ticked boxes. Concentrate on those where you have not yet been able to put a date in the "Date completed" column. The job is not finished until there is a "Date completed" entry on every line where you have ticked the box.

Things to check	Does this apply?	Guide page no	Notes/Action	Date completed
AA	☐	24	....	....
Accountant	☐	27	....	....
Allowances and Benefits (Child, Maternity, etc)	☐	20	....	....
Bank	L ☐	27	....	....
Blood Transfusion Service	☐	26	....	....
Borough Council – see Rates; Refuse Collection				
Book Club/ Other Postal Clubs	☐	24	....	....
British Rail – see Season Tickets				
Budget Accounts – see Charge Accounts				
Building Society	☐	27	....	....
Car Insurance – see Insurance, Motor Vehicle				
Car Parking Permit	☐	24	....	....
Charge Accounts	☐	28	....	....
Charities/Societies, eg National Trust, OXFAM	☐	24	....	....
Clubs, Sports/Social/Community	☐	24	....	....

Things to check	Does this apply?	Guide page no	Notes/Action	Date completed
Community Charge ("Poll Tax")	☐	21	....	....
Credit Card Companies, eg Access, Visa	☐	27	....	....
Credit Notes	☐	30	....	....
DSS (Department of Social Security) – see Allowances and Benefits				
Dangerous Animals	☐	19	....	....
Dentist	☐	26	....	....
District Council – see Rates; Refuse Collection				
Doctor	☐	26	....	....
Dog Licence	☐	19	....	....
Driving Licence	☐	24	....	....
Dry Cleaning	☐	30	....	....
DVLC – see Driving Licence; Motor Vehicle Licence				
Electoral Register	☐	18	....	....
Electricity Board	L☐	18	....	....
Employers	☐	25	....	....

Things to check	Does this apply?	Guide page no	Notes/Action	Date completed
Equipment Maintenance – see Service Contracts				
Finance House – see Hire/Lease Purchase				
Firearms/Shotguns	☐	25	....	....
Football Pools	☐	24	....	....
Friendly Societies	☐	24	....	....
Fuel (Oil/Coal)	☐	28	....	....
Gas Company	L ☐	18	....	....
Hire/Lease Purchase	☐	28	....	....
Hospital	☐	26	....	....
Household Equipment Repairs	☐	30	....	....
Housing Benefit	☐	25	....	....
Income Support – see Unemployment Benefit				
Inland Revenue	☐	27	....	....
Insurance			....	....
– Broker	☐	27	....	....
– House and Contents	☐	28	....	....
– Health	☐	29	....	....
– Life	☐	29	....	....
– Motor Vehicle	☐	29	....	....
– Other	☐	29	....	....

Things to check	Does this apply?	Guide page no	Notes/Action	Date completed
Kidney/Organ Donor	☐	26	....	....
Library	☐	26	....	....
Licences – Dangerous Animals, Dogs, Driving, Motor Vehicle, Television – see individual headings				
Magazines – see Periodicals				
Mail Order Houses	☐	28	....	....
Mail Redirection	☐	19	....	....
Milk Delivery	☐	30	....	....
Monthly Accounts – see Charge Accounts				
Motor Vehicle Licence	☐	24	....	....
National Insurance – see Allowances and Benefits				
Newsagent	☐	30	....	....
Optician	☐	26	....	....
Passport Office	☐	26	....	....
Pension			....	....
– private	☐	27	....	....
– state retirement	☐	27	....	....
Periodicals	☐	28	....	....

Things to check	Does this apply?	Guide page no	Notes/Action	Date completed
Pets	☐	19	....	....
Photographs	☐	30	....	....
Poll Tax – see Community Charge				
Post – see Mail Redirection				
Post Office – Mail Redirection, TV Licence, Premium Bonds, and National Savings – see individual headings				
Postal Vote – see Electoral Register				
Premium Bonds and National Savings	☐	20	....	....
Professional Institutions	☐	24	....	....
RAC	☐	24	....	....
Rates	L☐	21	....	....
Record Club	☐	24	....	....
Refuse Collection	☐	22	....	....
Schools	☐	22	....	....
Season Tickets	☐	23	....	....
Service Contracts (Equipment)	☐	29	....	....

Things to check	Does this apply?	Guide page no	Notes/Action	Date completed
Shareholdings – see Stockbroker				
Shoe Repairs	☐	30	....	....
Shotguns - see Firearms/Shotguns				
Solicitor	☐	27	....	....
Stockbroker/Stocks and Shares	☐	27	....	....
Tax Inspector	☐	27	....	....
Telephone	L☐	22	....	....
Television Licence	☐	20	....	....
Television and Video Rental	L☐	29	....	....
Theatre Bookings	☐	30	....	....
Trade Unions	☐	24	....	
Travel Agent	☐	30	....	....
Unemployment Benefit	☐	27	....	....
Veterinary Practice – see Pets				
Video Rental - see Television				
Water	L☐	23	....	....

The Guide

General Services 18

Electoral Register (your vote) 18
Electricity 18
Gas 18
Pets 19
Post Office Facilities
  Redirection of Mail 19
  Television Licence 20
  Allowances and Benefits 20
  Premium Bonds 20
  Other National Savings 21
Rates 21
Refuse Collection 22
Schools 22
Telephone 22
Water 18

Individual Services 23

British Rail Season Tickets 23
Car Parking Permit 24
Clubs and Societies 24
Driving Licence and Vehicle Registration Document 24
Employers 25
Firearms/Shotguns 25
Housing Benefit 25
Library 26
Passport 26
Professional Services
  Medical and Dental 26
  Financial and Legal 27
Unemployment Benefit/Income Support 27

Business and Commercial Services 28

Charge Accounts 28
Hire/Lease Purchase Agreements 28
Insurance
  House (Building and Contents) Insurance 28
  Motor Vehicle Insurance 29
  Other Insurance Policies 29
Service Contracts (Equipment) 29
Television and Video Rental 29

A Final Miscellany 30

General Services

Electoral Register (your vote)

The current Electoral Register cannot be amended to take account of your change of address. If you are unable to return to your polling station to vote at any election or by-election you can obtain the necessary forms to apply for a postal vote from the Electoral Registration Officer of the District/Borough Council where you are currently registered.

Note: You must apply for a postal vote each time you wish to vote. It is most important that you apply for a postal vote as soon as an election or by-election date is known as any delay could result in your losing your right to vote by post.

The Register is revised annually and is based on your place of residence on October 10th each year. If you move into your new home on or before that date, but after the annual Register of Electors form (Form A) is distributed (usually at the end of August), you should apply to the Electoral Registration Office of your new district to ensure that your name is included in the next year's register.

Electricity, Gas, Water

On the assumption that the property you are selling and the one you are buying are supplied with one or more of these main services, you will need to ensure that you pay for them only to the extent that you are legally or contractually liable. You must therefore notify the services of the dates when you are to complete the sale of your present house and the purchase of your new house.

Any "Budget Plan" or similar arrangement you may have for paying your bills will be terminated when you change your address and you will probably be required to pay whatever sum may be outstanding up to that date (or you will be paid any credit balance due to you). You will probably want to apply for similar arrangements for paying your bills in future. Remember to ask about this when you apply for the service to be available in your new home.

You will, of course, need to arrange for gas and electricity meters to be read (also, if you have one, the water meter). It will also be necessary to arrange for domestic appliances, eg gas cooker, washing machine, to be disconnected and reconnected at your new house. This may be done by the supplier's own staff, or, perhaps more economically, by securing the services of a local domestic service engineer (see Yellow Pages).

You can notify the appropriate companies or statutory authorities of your requirements by telephone or by writing. (In the case of your new house, you may be required to sign new contracts for the supply of these services.)

Any servicing agreements you may have for appliances that you plan to take with you will probably be terminated when you move. If you want to continue with similar servicing agreements, you will need to apply to the appropriate company.

If you are moving to a different area, you will normally be able to find out the addresses to write to from the estate agents through whom you are buying your house, or perhaps directly from the vendors themselves. Another source of this information is the Public Library Service, whose larger branches have telephone directories covering the whole country.

Don't forget that you may have to contact two different Water Authorities – a Water Supply Company and a Water Services Authority. Again, the estate agent should be able to help you with this – or you can contact the Local Authority (Council) in your new area.

Gas – see entry under Electricity, Gas, Water

Pets

There is a section on your Dog Licence for recording your change of address. Simply take it to your new Post Office when you arrive.

If you have a pet of a kind listed in the Dangerous Wild Animals Act (1976), your new premises (or, to be precise, the enclosure in which the animal is kept) have to be licensed. This is arranged with the Local Authority, who should be contacted before you move. There is a limit of 72 hours on the time the animal is allowed to be in transit.

If you have an insurance policy for your pet, be sure to inform the insurance company (or the vet, if he is acting as broker) of your change of address.

Perhaps you feel that your pet might be distressed during the process of moving house. In this case, it may be helpful if you have a friend who could look after it during the move. Alternatively, you could consider booking it into a boarding establishment. Your local authority will have a list of licensed establishments. There is also a section in the Yellow Pages under the heading "Boarding Kennels".

If you are moving a long distance, say more that a two-hour car journey, you may think it wise to seek veterinary advice as to the effect the journey may have on your pet, and the advisability or otherwise of tranquillisers/travel sickness pills. Incidentally, your vet may be able to recommend a colleague in the area to which you are moving.

The RSPCA (whose Head Office address is The Causeway, Horsham, West Sussex, RH12 1HG, telephone 0403 64181) is also available to give more advice about your pet's welfare.

Don't forget to give the new occupiers of your house a description of your pets – just in case they wander back "home"! (And change their name and address tags.)

Post Office Facilities

Redirection of Mail

A "Royal Mail Redirection Service" is available from the Post Office. Pick up Form P944 from any main Post Office, complete it, and return it at least one week before you move.

A fee is payable for this service according to the length of time you want your mail to be redirected. The current charges are:

Up to 1 calendar month – £2.75
Up to 3 calendar months – £6.25
Up to 12 calendar months – £15.00

Parcels sent by Letter Post are treated as letters under the Redirection Service. However, for parcels sent by Parcel Post, a surcharge is payable on delivery to the new address. This is generally equal to the postage paid, or, in the case of parcels from abroad, the equivalent UK parcel post rate from your old address.

You may think it a good idea to suggest to the people from whom you are buying your house that they make use of the Redirection Service – to save you the problem of dealing with mail arriving for them after you've moved in.

Note: Experience suggests that this service does not always work perfectly, and you are recommended to notify all those people and organisations who may write to you of your change of address as soon as possible.

Television Licence

The Post Office Form P944 (Mail Redirection) includes a section in which you can record new address details for your television licence. If you do not intend to use the Mail Redirection Service, you can take your current TV licence into any Post Office so that details may be transferred to your new address.

Allowances and Benefits

If you draw state allowances or benefits from your local Post Office you should take your allowance book to the Post Office in your new area where you want the future payments to be made. This can be arranged without delay. At some offices you may be asked to provide evidence of identity other than the allowance book itself.

The DSS (Department of Social Security) asks that you notify their local office before you move, so that your records can be transferred.

Premium Bonds

Premium bond holders should amend their Holder's Card and send it to the Bonds and Stock Office at the address printed on it. Alternatively, you can pick up a Change of Name/Address Form P2767B (and a pre-paid addressed envelope) from the Post Office to register your change of address.

Other National Savings

Holders should advise the appropriate office at the address shown on the bank, deposit, or account book, or on the security document, quoting full details of the account or holding.

Rates

It may be that you will have agreed with your solicitors that they will deal with all matters relating to your liability for rates. In this case you will only need to keep them informed about any changes in your plans regarding dates of moving in and out.

If, however, you are dealing with your rate payments yourself, you will want to ensure that you do not pay rates on your existing property beyond the date of completion of sale. Similarly, you will not want to pay rates on your new property until you are legally liable to do so. You must therefore inform both the old and new rating authority (usually the District Council) of the respective dates of completion of sale and completion of purchase. Remember that if you remove all your furniture from your old house before completion of sale, or if you delay moving your furniture into your new house until after completion of purchase, you may be in a position to claim a "void" period (ie a period when rates are not due to be paid) when a property you own is empty of furniture and not being occupied.

Note: Different authorities have different rules concerning the duration of the void period. Contact your local authority for policy details.

If you are moving to a different rating authority area, and you pay your rates by banker's order or by means of a direct debiting mandate, you should remember to cancel these instructions to your bank, and to advise the rating authority that you have done so, and from what date. The rating authority will then arrange to calculate the amount of rates due against the amount paid, and either send you a bill for the balance owing or a refund of the amount overpaid.

If you are moving to a property within your existing rating authority area you will need to amend your instructions to your bank, or, in the case of a direct debiting mandate, your authorisation to the Council. The Council will calculate the adjustments necessary, and advise you accordingly.

Note: The new Community Charge (often referred to as the "Poll Tax") is to replace the present rating system and is due to be introduced in Scotland in April 1989 and in England and Wales in April 1990. At the time of going to press, details are not available of the arrangements to be made for collecting this charge and for notifying changes of address. Contact your local rating authority for details.

Refuse Collection

You may wish to arrange with your local authority for a special refuse collection service to be provided when you move house. Many authorities will undertake to do this, provided reasonable notice is given.

If the property you are moving to has been unoccupied for some time you will need to notify your new local authority so that they can arrange regular refuse collection after you have moved in.

Schools

If you have school-going children, and you are moving to a different area, you will want to make sure that they transfer to the appropriate schools. You can obtain lists of state schools from the Local Education Authority of your new area, or possibly via the estate agent through whom you are buying your house.

It is recommended that you contact the school(s) in the new area well in advance of your move with a view to obtaining information on the admissions policy and on the individual schools themselves. It may also be possible to arrange a day visit for your children, in order to help the transition from one school to another.

You should also, or course, inform your children's present school(s) of their forthcoming departure. The staff may be able to offer advice on coping with the move to a new school and provide reports.

Telephone

You will want to ensure that you incur telephone charges (rental and called units) on your existing telephone only up to the date on which you leave your present home. You can either telephone or write to your British Telecom Area Office to arrange this. Don't forget that if you own any of the telephone equipment in your house, it is yours to take with you to your new house or to dispose of otherwise as you may wish.

As regards your new home, there are two main aspects which will concern you.

Firstly, there is the provision of the telephone connection (line) to the house. You may have the following options available:-

1 If there is a telephone connected to your new home, you may simply take over this line. The charge is currently £16.00. If, however, the telephone has been disconnected for more than three months, it will be treated as a new line (see para 3 below).

2 Alternatively, if you are moving within the same telephone exchange area, you may request the transfer of your existing telephone number to the new address. If the new house is already connected, the charge will be £21.00.

3 Finally, if there is no line already connected to your new house, the charge for installing a new one is £90.00 if you are already a telephone subscriber, or £105.00 if you are not. If you are moving to a particularly remote area, not served by a main telephone cable, you may be charged for installation work.

Should you wish to ensure that no unauthorised calls are made from your telephone (if, for instance, you arrange for various works to be carried out in your new house before you move in) you can ask British Telecom to apply the "Outgoing Calls Barred" service for whatever period you decide. This will cost you £11.00.

Incidentally, British Telecom will automatically apply this service to the telephone in your present house from the date you move out unless the new occupier makes other arrangements.

The second aspect of telephone provision is the installation in your new house. It is worth contacting the vendor to find out what equipment is already there. This includes the number, type, and location of the jackpoints or sockets for extension lines, the number and type of telephone instruments in the house (which are not the vendor's own personal property), answering machine sockets, etc. With this information you can decide on any modifications you need and arrange for them to be carried out promptly and economically.

You should remember to ask for new telephone directories. If you are moving to an "overlap" area, ie near the boundary of two British Telecom Telephone Areas, you can have directories for both areas free of charge. The Yellow Pages directory is only provided free for the area which includes your exchange. You may order other telephone directories and Yellow Pages directories from your British Telecom Area Sales Office.

Whatever your requirements, it is advisable to give British Telecom as much notice as possible. BT requires a minimum of eight working days' notice, although the installation of a new external line can take up to six weeks – longer in exceptional circumstances.

Liaison with the vendor of your new house (and, for that matter, with the buyer of your present house) can help you avoid the risk of incurring unnecessary disconnection, reconnection, or equipment replacement charges. It can also help prevent frustrating delays in getting your telephone system up and running in your new home.

Water – see entry under Electricity, Gas, Water

Individual Services

British Rail Season Tickets

If you have a British Rail season ticket which is unexpired on the date you move and you no longer need to use it, you can claim a refund for the unused period by returning it to the ISSUING station. Refunds against season tickets are not calculated on a pro rata basis. You will be asked to complete a form requesting either a refund or a "Changeover" (change of route). BR suggest that there may be a delay of 14 days before you receive your refund. There may also be a similar delay for any refund due on a Changeover.

Car Parking Permit

If you have a car parking permit issued by your local authority, you will normally be entitled to a refund of any fee paid from the date you return it to them. This could take a few weeks in some areas.

If you need a permit for your new location (assuming your new local authority issues such permits), you should write to them with details of your new address. Apply as soon as possible because the allocation of new permits can take some time.

Note: You may be moving to or from a street with difficult or restricted parking. It is customary in many areas to apply in advance to the local authority for a reserved parking zone outside the house on the day of the move. This is generally done by the removals contractors but it may be an idea to check that they have made these arrangements – you don't want to be unpopular with your new neighbours from the day you move in!

Clubs, Societies, Trade Unions

You may belong to a number of different clubs, societies, trade unions, and other organisations. These could include:-

motoring organisations (eg AA, RAC)
book, record, video clubs
charities (eg OXFAM)
leisure interest organisations (eg National Trust)
professional institutions
special interest groups (eg RSPCA)
sports/social clubs
political parties
sectarian associations
trade unions
adult education classes (eg Open University, Open College)
community/residents' groups
parent/teacher associations
football pools
friendly societies

You will want to notify them of your change of address to ensure that literature, notices, membership cards, and goods ordered will be correctly delivered to your new home and, if appropriate, so that you can be sent details of club activities or facilities in your new area.

Driving Licence and Vehicle Registration Document

You are required by law to notify the Driver and Vehicle Licensing Centre if any of the details shown on your driving licence or vehicle registration document (V5) are incorrect. Both these documents contain sections which you will need to complete to notify the DVLC of details like a change of address. You are advised to read the instructions carefully.

There are penalties for failing to notify the DVLC of changes to personal details. Maximum penalties are £400 for driving licence offences and £100 for vehicle registration offences.

Driving Licences should be sent to DVLC, Swansea, SA99 1BN, whilst Vehicle Registration Documents should be sent to DVLC, Swansea, SA99 1AR.

Note: The difference in postcode is important. The DVLC requests you to make sure that you use the correct one.

Employers

Whether or not moving home means changing your job as well, you will need to ensure that your employers know your new address. They may need to send you documents at home and also record the details of your address in connection with, for example, a company pension scheme. If you change your bank, they will need to know the address of the new branch in order to arrange payment of salary, pension, etc.

Firearms/Shotguns

If you hold a shotgun certificate or a firearms certificate you should ensure that it is amended when you change your address. In the case of a firearms certificate issued under the "Firearms Act (1968)", it is an offence if your current address is not shown on the certificate and you could pay a fine of up to £2,000 or even be jailed for up to six months if you forget to have your certificate amended by the issuing authority – usually the county police firearms department.

Another condition of issue of a firearms certificate concerns the secure safe-keeping of the weapon(s) and you will need to make sure that this condition is satisfied in your new home.

In the case of either a shotgun or a firearm certificate, you should send your certificate to the issuing authority – or take it to your local police station – with a note of your new address. Their records will be amended, and a new or amended certificate will be sent to you. If you are moving to a different police authority area, the issuing authority will notify the new one, who will be responsible for issuing a new or amended certificate.

Housing Benefit

If you are claiming Housing Benefit from your local authority/council, you should notify them of your change of address. You may need to make a new claim in respect of your new address.

Library

Remember to return all your library books, music tapes, pictures, or anything else you have on loan from you library. (It may be possible to take them with you for a time to your new address, but you would need to ask your librarian first.)

If your library has a computerised ticketing system, your ticket will normally be valid at another computerised library if you are moving within the same County or Borough. Your new library will still need to know your new address.

Passport

You may consider it desirable, although it is not obligatory, to advise the Passport Office of your change of address in case it should ever be necessary for your home to be contacted by means of your passport. You should write to the Passport Office covering your home area (address obtainable from the Post Office), and quote your name, your passport number, and your new and old addresses.

Professional Services – Medical, Legal, Financial

Medical and Dental

If you are moving away from your existing area, and your doctor is not prepared to treat you at your new address, you will need to register with another doctor (assuming that you are a National Health Service patient). A list of NHS doctors can be obtained from the Family Practitioner Committee of your new area (address in the telephone directory). Take your medical card to the doctor of your choice. If he or she accepts you as a patient he will inform the Family Practitioner Committee who will make arrangements for the transfer of your record. (This may take several weeks – or even months.) If you have difficulty in finding a doctor, contact the local FPC.

You are not registered with a dentist in the same way as with a doctor. If you need to find a dentist in your new area, however, the FPC will be able to help you with the names and addresses of local dentists. Acceptance by a new dentist does not involve a transfer of records as in the case of a change of doctor.

It would be courteous to advise both your doctor and your dentist of your coming change of address.

In the same way, you may wish to advise your optician (if you have one) and your local hospital or clinic (if you have been, or are, a patient). They should be able to help you with names and addresses of hospitals and clinics in your new area.

Finally, if you are a blood donor, remember to notify the regional office of the National Blood Transfusion Service so that they will be able to send you details of the local visits programme at your new address. Also, if you hold a kidney or organ donor card, and the person named on it as your contact is also moving house, remember to amend his/her telephone number on the card.

Financial and Legal

Holders of credit cards (ACCESS, VISA, American Express, etc) should notify the issuing organisations of any change of address, not only in order to ensure that the monthly bills are sent to the new address, but also in case contact needs to be made in the event of loss, theft, or fraudulent use of the card.

If you receive a state pension and are moving to a different area, you should call at the Post Office where you want your pension to be paid to record your change of address. Ask for form P80MA (Pension or Allowances – Change of Post Office and/or Address form), complete it, and hand it in. Your pension will be payable at the new Post Office right away.

Should you be in receipt of a private pension, it is in your interest to advise the paying office of your new address without delay, whether or not the pension is credited to a bank account. You may have entitlement to a deferred pension (ie a pension not due to be paid until some time in the future). You should notify the pension fund office of your change of address.

Perhaps you have dealings with a solicitor other than the one helping you with selling and buying your house – someone who holds some important documents (eg a will) or who is dealing with some other legal matters for you.

Moving house could well require changes to be made to standing orders and direct debiting mandates operated through your bank account. Advise the bank accordingly.

You may also use the services of an accountant, a stockbroker, and/or an insurance broker. If you own shares you will need to ensure that the registrars of the companies concerned are advised of your new address. You may have an account with a building society which is not involved in your house move.

All these professional bodies and people need to be advised of your change of address...and, by the way, don't forget your tax inspector!

Unemployment Benefit/Income Support

If you are claiming Unemployment Benefit and/or Income Support through the Unemployment Benefit Office and you are moving within the same area, you should go to the UBO where you will be requested to fill in a form with your new address and choice of Post Office where you would like to cash your cheques.

If you are moving to a different area, you must go to the new UBO as soon as you have moved in and make a new claim. Your records will be automatically transferred from the old office.

Business and Commercial Services

Charge Accounts

You may have a number of accounts with different businesses – local retail shops, car servicing garages, department stores, fuel delivery firms, mail order companies, or publishers of periodicals and journals. Tell them that you are moving and either ask for your outstanding account to be sent to you for settlement, or for the account to be continued at your new address. Remember that an unpaid account (if, for instance, it was sent to your old address and not forwarded to you) may result in difficulties in securing credit in the future.

Hire/Lease Purchase Agreements

Perhaps you have a Hire or Lease Purchase Agreement for your car, personal computer, dishwasher, dining room suite, etc. The finance house will need to know the new location of the items involved and may possibly require confirmation that they will continue to be covered by insurance.

Insurance

House (Building and Contents) Insurance

When you exchange contracts you become responsible for your new house and you should make sure that you are properly insured from that date. You should check the requirements of your mortgage provider (eg Building Society, insurance company, bank) regarding "buildings" insurance – the sum to be insured, the effective date, and what the policy covers.

Your solicitors will probably arrange this for you. Many Building Societies prefer you to insure with their recommended insurers. This is not a legal requirement, but you may have to pay an "administration charge" if you want to insure with another company (for instance, if you want to continue with your existing insurance company).

You will also need to consider amending your "contents" insurance policy. Notify the insurers that the cover should be transferred to the new address on the day you move. You may need to modify the amount of cover (up or down) according to whether you are buying or selling furniture and household effects when you move. The insurance company may vary the rate of premium according to the type of house and the district you are moving into.

Note: Do not forget to arrange for your house contents to be adequately insured in transit from your old to your new house (and while being loaded and unloaded). Also, of course, it is necessary to make special arrangements in the event of furniture being left in a furniture depository. This may be done through a removals contractor or your own insurance company. Insurance cover will not normally cover "fragile" articles unless they are packed by the removals contractor's own staff. Take care, therefore, if you decide to "help" by packing your own valuable china!

Motor Vehicle Insurance

You will also need to notify your motor insurance company (or broker) of your new address in order to ensure continuation of cover. The premium you pay may be affected by the change of district in which you live and "off-the-road" garaging facilities at your new home.

Other Insurance Policies

Make sure you notify all the insurance companies (or a broker if you use one) with whom you hold other insurance policies (eg life, health, professional indemnity, dangerous sports, etc). The validity of some policies may be affected if you do not notify change of address.

Service Contracts (Equipment)

If you have a contract to cover the servicing and repair of household appliances, eg a washing machine, you will need to discuss with the servicing organisation the position after you move house. In cases where a national servicing organisation is involved, it may be possible to continue the contract at your new address. Check your contract and advise the service organisation accordingly.

Television and Video Rental

If you rent your television and/or video equipment, you will need to make arrangements to cater for your move. National rental companies will normally be able to arrange for you to take your equipment to the new address and for service to be provided locally. If, however, you rent from a local firm, you may find that you have to terminate your rental agreement, return the equipment, and take out a new agreement with a supplier in your new area. Check your rental agreement and contact the rental firm if you have any doubt about your position.

A Final Miscellany

Check through your wallets, handbags, desk drawers, and behind the clock on the mantelpiece in the lounge. You may have receipts for clothes at the cleaners, your watch which is being repaired, or a credit note which you haven't yet redeemed. Have you booked and paid a deposit on a holiday with a local travel agent? Have you ordered some theatre tickets?

Here are some checkpoints:-

Photograph developers
Shoe repairers
Dry cleaners
Travel agency
Theatre reservations
Milkman
Bookshop orders
Video club
Newsagent
Household equipment repairs

Experience suggests that, whether you notify the main service-provider organisations (eg electricity board, gas company, British Telecom) by letter or by telephone, it is advisable to double-check after, say, two weeks to make sure that your message has been received and understood, and that the appropriate action is in hand.

The Letters

Specialised pre-printed letters for mailing to the following suppliers of goods and services:

Duplicate Letters

ELECTRICITY BOARD
GAS COMPANY
RATES (DISTRICT/BOROUGH COUNCIL)
TELEPHONE (BRITISH TELECOM)
WATER SERVICES AUTHORITY
WATER SUPPLY COMPANY

Single Letters

BANK
MOTOR INSURANCE COMPANY
TV/VIDEO RENTAL COMPANY

"Open" Letters

A set of "open" letters for mailing to other organisations

Duplicate Letters

These six letters are in duplicate. They are addressed to those organisations which provide basic household services – electricity, gas, water supply, water services, telephone, and the rating authority. These letters are in duplicate because, if you are moving to a different area, you will need to notify the organisations in your existing area that you are moving out and those in your new area that you are moving in.

If, however, you are moving to an address which is covered by the same branch or area office of the organisation concerned, then only one letter is necessary. You may not know whether your new property is served by the same office. You can usually find this out from the vendor's estate agent or, if necessary, you can telephone the office you normally deal with (you will find the telephone number on your last bill).

Complete the duplicate letters as follows:-

If you are Moving to a Different Area

Use one copy of the letter to send to the office of the organisation which deals with your present account. COMPLETE SECTION 1 and DELETE SECTION 2.

Use the other copy for the office which covers your new address. COMPLETE SECTION 2 and DELETE SECTION 1.

If you are Moving within the Same Area

Use only one copy of the letter and send it to the office which deals with your present account. COMPLETE BOTH SECTIONS 1 and 2.

Note 1: Because the service areas of different organisations are not the same, you may find that you have to notify, for example, two different rating authority districts, but only one electricity board office.

Note 2: If you currently pay bills to both a water supply company and a water services authority (for sewerage and environmental services) you will have to notify both these organisations that you are moving. You will need to find out (probably via the vendor's estate agent) whether water supply and water services organisations in your new area bill their customers separately, and notify them accordingly.

Single Letters

These letters are intended for your bank, your motor insurance company, and your TV/Video company, and are designed to help you provide the information these organisations need to have about your move.

"Open" Letters

These letters can be used for communicating your change of address to any other organisations which you need to notify.

All the pre-printed letters which follow are easily removed from the book by tearing along the perforated line.

ELECTRICITY

NOTIFICATION OF CHANGE OF ADDRESS

From:
Address:

Telephone no: Date:

To: The Electricity Board
Address:

Dear Sir/Madam,

NOTIFICATION OF CHANGE OF ADDRESS

This is to notify you of my/our change of address as follows:

Date of moving out of the above address:

New address:

New telephone no: Date of moving in:

SECTION 1: METER READING – Present Address:

re: Account Reference No:

Please arrange to read the meter at my/our present address (see above) in the morning/afternoon on ....

*Please also arrange to disconnect the equipment indicated below at the same time:

SECTION 2: METER READING – New Address:

Please ensure that electricity supply is available and/or arrange to read the meter at my/our new address (see above) in the morning/afternoon on..

*Please also arrange to reconnect the equipment indicated below at the same time:

Yours faithfully ....

EQUIPMENT (delete or add as necessary)
electric cooker other equipment (specify) ....

*delete if not applicable

ELECTRICITY

NOTIFICATION OF CHANGE OF ADDRESS

From:
Address:

Telephone no: Date:

To: The Electricity Board
Address:

Dear Sir/Madam,

NOTIFICATION OF CHANGE OF ADDRESS

This is to notify you of my/our change of address as follows:

Date of moving out of the above address:

New address:

New telephone no: Date of moving in:

SECTION 1: METER READING – Present Address:

re: Account Reference No:

Please arrange to read the meter at my/our present address (see above) in the morning/afternoon on ....

*Please also arrange to disconnect the equipment indicated below at the same time:

SECTION 2: METER READING – New Address:

Please ensure that electricity supply is available and/or arrange to read the meter at my/our new address (see above) in the morning/afternoon on ....

*Please also arrange to reconnect the equipment indicated below at the same time:

Yours faithfully ....

EQUIPMENT (delete or add as necessary)

electric cooker other equipment (specify) ....

*delete if not applicable

GAS

NOTIFICATION OF CHANGE OF ADDRESS

From:
Address:

Telephone no: Date:

To: British Gas
Address:

Dear Sir/Madam,

NOTIFICATION OF CHANGE OF ADDRESS

This is to notify you of my/our change of address as follows:
Date of moving out of the above address:
New address:

New telephone no: Date of moving in:

SECTION 1: METER READING – Present Address:

re: Account Reference No:

Please arrange to read the meter at my/our present address (see above) in the morning/afternoon on ....

*Please also arrange to disconnect the equipment indicated below at the same time:

SECTION 2: METER READING – New Address:

Please ensure that gas supply is available and/or arrange to read the meter at my/our new address (see above) in the morning/afternoon on ....

*Please also arrange to reconnect the equipment indicated below at the same time:

*delete if not applicable

Yours faithfully ....

EQUIPMENT (delete or add as necessary)
gas cooker
gas fire(s) other equipment (specify) ....

GAS

NOTIFICATION OF CHANGE OF ADDRESS

From:
Address:

Telephone no: Date:

To: British Gas
Address:

Dear Sir/Madam,

NOTIFICATION OF CHANGE OF ADDRESS

This is to notify you of my/our change of address as follows:
Date of moving out of the above address:
New address:

New telephone no: Date of moving in:

SECTION 1: METER READING – Present Address:

re: Account Reference No:

Please arrange to read the meter at my/our present address (see above) in the morning/afternoon on ....

*Please also arrange to disconnect the equipment indicated below at the same time:

SECTION 2: METER READING – New Address:

Please ensure that gas supply is available and/or arrange to read the meter at my/our new address (see above) in the morning/afternoon on ....

*Please also arrange to reconnect the equipment indicated below at the same time:

*delete if not applicable

Yours faithfully ....

EQUIPMENT (delete or add as necessary)
gas cooker
gas fire(s) other equipment (specify) ....

RATES

NOTIFICATION OF CHANGE OF ADDRESS

From:
Address:

Telephone no: Date:

To: The Rates Office
Name of Council and Address:

Dear Sir/Madam,

NOTIFICATION OF CHANGE OF ADDRESS

This is to notify you of my/our change of address as follows:

New address:

New telephone no:

SECTION 1: PAYMENT OF RATES – TERMINATION

Rates Reference No:

Date of completion of sale of my/our present property:

No further payment of rates will be made in respect of my/our present address (see above) unless or until a statment of rates due is received. Alternatively, I/we claim repayment of any rates overpaid.

SECTION 2: PAYMENT OF RATES – COMMENCEMENT

Date of completion of purchase of my/our new property:

Please send me/us details of rates due in respect of my/our new address (see above), and alternative methods of payment.

Yours faithfully ....

RATES

NOTIFICATION OF CHANGE OF ADDRESS

From:
Address:

Telephone no: Date:

To: The Rates Office
Name of Council and Address:

Dear Sir/Madam,

NOTIFICATION OF CHANGE OF ADDRESS

This is to notify you of my/our change of address as follows:

New address:

New telephone no:

SECTION 1: PAYMENT OF RATES – TERMINATION

Rates Reference No:

Date of completion of sale of my/our present property:

No further payment of rates will be made in respect of my/our present address (see above) unless or until a statment of rates due is received. Alternatively, I/we claim repayment of any rates overpaid.

SECTION 2: PAYMENT OF RATES – COMMENCEMENT

Date of completion of purchase of my/our new property:

Please send me/us details of rates due in respect of my/our new address (see above), and alternative methods of payment.

Yours faithfully ....

TELEPHONE
NOTIFICATION OF CHANGE OF ADDRESS

From:
Address:

Telephone no: Date:

To: British Telecom plc
Address:

Dear Sir/Madam,

NOTIFICATION OF CHANGE OF ADDRESS

This is to notify you of my/our change of address as follows:

Date of moving out of the above address:

New address:

New telephone no:

Date of moving in:

SECTION 1: PRESENT TELEPHONE SERVICE:

Please arrange to provide an account for rental charges and calls made up to......................am/pm on the date of leaving my/our present address (see above).

SECTION 2: NEW TELEPHONE SERVICE

Please arrange to:*
a) install a new telephone line
b) open the line already installed
c) transfer my/our existing telephone number to my/ our new address on the date of moving in (see above)
*delete as appropriate

Yours faithfully ....

TELEPHONE

NOTIFICATION OF CHANGE OF ADDRESS

From:
Address:

Telephone no: Date:

To: British Telecom plc
Address:

Dear Sir/Madam,

NOTIFICATION OF CHANGE OF ADDRESS

This is to notify you of my/our change of address as follows:

Date of moving out of the above address:

New address:

New telephone no:

Date of moving in:

SECTION 1: PRESENT TELEPHONE SERVICE:

Please arrange to provide an account for rental charges and calls made up to...................... am/pm on the date of leaving my/our present address (see above).

SECTION 2: NEW TELEPHONE SERVICE

Please arrange to:*
a) install a new telephone line
b) open the line already installed
c) transfer my/our existing telephone number to my/ our new address on the date of moving in (see above)

*delete as appropriate

Yours faithfully ....

Telephone; Date sent..

WATER SERVICES

NOTIFICATION OF CHANGE OF ADDRESS

From:
Address:

Telephone no: Date:

To: The Water Services Authority
Address:

Dear Sir/Madam,

NOTIFICATION OF CHANGE OF ADDRESS

This is to notify you of my/our change of address as follows:

New address:

New telephone no:

SECTION 1: PAYMENT OF WATER SERVICES ACCOUNT – TERMINATION

re: Water Services Account Reference No:

Date of completion of sale of my/our present property:

No further payment of rates will be made in respect of my/our present address (see above) unless or until a statment of charges due is received. Alternatively, I/we claim repayment of any charges overpaid.

SECTION 2: PAYMENT OF WATER SERVICES ACCOUNT – COMMENCEMENT

Date of completion of purchase of my/our new property:

Please send me/us details of charges due in respect of my/our new address (see above), and alternative methods of payment.

Yours faithfully ....

Water Services Authority; Date sent..

WATER SERVICES

NOTIFICATION OF CHANGE OF ADDRESS

From:
Address:

Telephone no: Date:

To: The Water Services Authority
Address:

Dear Sir/Madam,

NOTIFICATION OF CHANGE OF ADDRESS

This is to notify you of my/our change of address as follows:

New address:

New telephone no:

SECTION 1: PAYMENT OF WATER SERVICES ACCOUNT – TERMINATION

re: Water Services Account Reference No:

Date of completion of sale of my/our present property:

No further payment of rates will be made in respect of my/our present address (see above) unless or until a statment of charges due is received. Alternatively, I/we claim repayment of any charges overpaid.

SECTION 2: PAYMENT OF WATER SERVICES ACCOUNT – COMMENCEMENT

Date of completion of purchase of my/our new property:

Please send me/us details of charges due in respect of my/our new address (see above), and alternative methods of payment.

Yours faithfully ....

Water Services Authority, Date sent

WATER SUPPLY

NOTIFICATION OF CHANGE OF ADDRESS

From:
Address:

Telephone no: Date:

To: The Water Supply Company
Address:

Dear Sir/Madam,

NOTIFICATION OF CHANGE OF ADDRESS

This is to notify you of my/our change of address as follows

New address:

New telephone no:

SECTION 1: PAYMENT OF WATER SUPPLY ACCOUNT – TERMINATION

re: Water Supply Account Reference No.:

Date of completion of sale of my/our present property:

No further payment of rates will be made in respect of my/our present address (see above) unless or until a statment of charges due is received. Alternatively, I/we claim repayment of any charges overpaid.

*Please arrange to read the meter not later than ...am/pm on ....

SECTION 2: PAYMENT OF WATER SUPPLY ACCOUNT – COMMENCEMENT

Date of completion of purchase of my/our new property:

Please send me/us details of charges due in respect of my/our new address (see above), and alternative methods of payment.

*delete if not applicable

Yours faithfully ....

Water Supply Company; Date sent..

WATER SUPPLY

NOTIFICATION OF CHANGE OF ADDRESS

From:
Address:

Telephone no: Date:

To: The Water Supply Company
Address:

Dear Sir/Madam,

NOTIFICATION OF CHANGE OF ADDRESS

This is to notify you of my/our change of address as follows

New address:

New telephone no:

SECTION 1: PAYMENT OF WATER SUPPLY ACCOUNT – TERMINATION

re: Water Supply Account Reference No.:

Date of completion of sale of my/our present property:

No further payment of rates will be made in respect of my/our present address (see above) unless or until a statment of charges due is received. Alternatively, I/we claim repayment of any charges overpaid.

*Please arrange to read the meter not later than ...am/pm on ....

SECTION 2: PAYMENT OF WATER SUPPLY ACCOUNT – COMMENCEMENT

Date of completion of purchase of my/our new property:

Please send me/us details of charges due in respect of my/our new address (see above), and alternative methods of payment.

*delete if not applicable

Yours faithfully ....

Water Supply Company; Date sent: ....

BANK

NOTIFICATION OF CHANGE OF ADDRESS

From:
Address:

Date:

To: The Manager
Bank:
Address:

Dear Sir/Madam,

NOTIFICATION OF CHANGE OF ADDRESS

This is to notify you of my/our change of address as follows:

Date of moving out of the above address:

New address:

New telephone no:

Date of moving in:

DESCRIPTION OF ACCOUNTS HELD

Ac No ....

Names(s) of Accountholder(s) ....

Type of Account...

Ac No ....

Names(s) of Accountholder(s) ....

Type of Account...

continued over

CANCELLATION OF STANDING ORDERS

Please arrange to cancel the following standing orders:

Ac no ....

Payee..

Date of last payment ....

Ac no ....

Payee..

Date of last payment ....

Ac no ....

Payee..

Date of last payment ....

Yours faithfully ....

MOTOR INSURANCE

NOTIFICATION OF CHANGE OF ADDRESS

From:
Address:

Telephone no: Date:

To: Motor Policy Department
Company:
Address:

Dear Sir/Madam,

NOTIFICATION OF CHANGE OF ADDRESS

This is to notify you of my/our change of address as follows.

Date of moving out of the above address:

New address:

New telephone no:

Date of moving in:

DETAILS OF MOTOR INSURANCE POLICY/POLICIES

Policy no ....

Policy holder(s) ....

Vehicle registration no ....

Please advice me/us if there are any changes in policy premiums arising from this change of address.

Yours faithfully ....

TV/VIDEO RENTAL

NOTIFICATION OF CHANGE OF ADDRESS

From:
Address:

Telephone no: Date:

To: The Accounts Office
Company:
Address:

Dear Sir/Madam,

NOTIFICATION OF CHANGE OF ADDRESS

This is to notify you of my/our change of address as follows.

Date of moving out of the above address:

New address:

New telephone no:

Date of moving in:

*SECTION 1: CANCELLATION OF AGREEMENT

Please cancel my/our rental agreement with effect from the date of removal from my/our present address (see above). Please arrange to collect the equipment covered by the agreement not later than.....am/pm
on..

*SECTION 2: REMOVAL OF RENTED EQUIPMENT TO NEW ADDRESS

I/we wish to remove the equipment covered by my/our rental agreement to my/our new address (see above). Please provide details of your branch nearest to my/our new address, and forward new agreement forms if necessary.

*delete Section 1 or 2 as appropriate

Yours faithfully ....

NOTIFICATION OF CHANGE OF ADDRESS

From:
Address:

Telephone no:

Date:

To:
Address:

Dear Sir/Madam,

NOTIFICATION OF CHANGE OF ADDRESS

re: Reference/Account/Policy/Membership/Licence No:..

This is to notify you of my/our change of address as follows:

Date of moving out of the above address:

New address:

New telephone no:

Date of moving in:

Would you please amend your records accordingly.

Thank you.

Yours faithfully ....

NOTIFICATION OF CHANGE OF ADDRESS

From:
Address:

Telephone no:

Date:

To:
Address:

Dear Sir/Madam,

NOTIFICATION OF CHANGE OF ADDRESS

re: Reference/Account/Policy/Membership/Licence No:...

This is to notify you of my/our change of address as follows:

Date of moving out of the above address:

New address:

New telephone no:

Date of moving in:

Would you please amend your records accordingly.

Thank you.

Yours faithfully ....

NOTIFICATION OF CHANGE OF ADDRESS

From:
Address:

Telephone no:

Date:

To:
Address:

Dear Sir/Madam,

NOTIFICATION OF CHANGE OF ADDRESS

re: Reference/Account/Policy/Membership/Licence No:...

This is to notify you of my/our change of address as follows:

Date of moving out of the above address:

New address:

New telephone no:

Date of moving in:

Would you please amend your records accordingly.

Thank you.

Yours faithfully ....

Details..........

NOTIFICATION OF CHANGE OF ADDRESS

From:
Address:

Telephone no:

Date:

To:
Address:

Dear Sir/Madam,

NOTIFICATION OF CHANGE OF ADDRESS

re: Reference/Account/Policy/Membership/Licence No:..

This is to notify you of my/our change of address as follows:

Date of moving out of the above address:

New address:

New telephone no:

Date of moving in:

Would you please amend your records accordingly.

Thank you.

Yours faithfully ....

NOTIFICATION OF CHANGE OF ADDRESS

From:
Address:

Telephone no:

Date:

To:
Address:

Dear Sir/Madam,

NOTIFICATION OF CHANGE OF ADDRESS

re: Reference/Account/Policy/Membership/Licence No:..

This is to notify you of my/our change of address as follows:

Date of moving out of the above address:

New address:

New telephone no:

Date of moving in:

Would you please amend your records accordingly.

Thank you.

Yours faithfully ....

Details..

NOTIFICATION OF CHANGE OF ADDRESS

From:
Address:

Telephone no:

Date:

To:
Address:

Dear Sir/Madam,

NOTIFICATION OF CHANGE OF ADDRESS

re: Reference/Account/Policy/Membership/Licence No:..

This is to notify you of my/our change of address as follows:

Date of moving out of the above address:

New address:

New telephone no:

Date of moving in:

Would you please amend your records accordingly.

Thank you.

Yours faithfully ....

NOTIFICATION OF CHANGE OF ADDRESS

From:
Address:

Telephone no:

Date:

To:
Address:

Dear Sir/Madam,

NOTIFICATION OF CHANGE OF ADDRESS

re: Reference/Account/Policy/Membership/Licence No:..

This is to notify you of my/our change of address as follows:

Date of moving out of the above address:

New address:

New telephone no:

Date of moving in:

Would you please amend your records accordingly.

Thank you.

Yours faithfully ....

NOTIFICATION OF CHANGE OF ADDRESS

From:
Address:

Telephone no:

Date:

To:
Address:

Dear Sir/Madam,

NOTIFICATION OF CHANGE OF ADDRESS

re: Reference/Account/Policy/Membership/Licence No:..

This is to notify you of my/our change of address as follows:

Date of moving out of the above address:

New address:

New telephone no:

Date of moving in:

Would you please amend your records accordingly.

Thank you.

Yours faithfully ....

NOTIFICATION OF CHANGE OF ADDRESS

From:
Address:

Telephone no:

Date:

To:
Address:

Dear Sir/Madam,

NOTIFICATION OF CHANGE OF ADDRESS

re: Reference/Account/Policy/Membership/Licence No:..

This is to notify you of my/our change of address as follows:

Date of moving out of the above address:

New address:

New telephone no:

Date of moving in:

Would you please amend your records accordingly.

Thank you.

Yours faithfully ....

Details..

NOTIFICATION OF CHANGE OF ADDRESS

From:
Address:

Telephone no:

Date:

To:
Address:

Dear Sir/Madam,

NOTIFICATION OF CHANGE OF ADDRESS

re: Reference/Account/Policy/Membership/Licence No:...

This is to notify you of my/our change of address as follows:

Date of moving out of the above address:

New address:

New telephone no:

Date of moving in:

Would you please amend your records accordingly.

Thank you.

Yours faithfully ....

Details..........

NOTIFICATION OF CHANGE OF ADDRESS

From:
Address:

Telephone no:

Date:

To:
Address:

Dear Sir/Madam,

NOTIFICATION OF CHANGE OF ADDRESS

re: Reference/Account/Policy/Membership/Licence No:..

This is to notify you of my/our change of address as follows:

Date of moving out of the above address:

New address:

New telephone no:

Date of moving in:

Would you please amend your records accordingly.

Thank you.

Yours faithfully ....

NOTIFICATION OF CHANGE OF ADDRESS

From:
Address:

Telephone no:

Date:

To:
Address:

Dear Sir/Madam,

NOTIFICATION OF CHANGE OF ADDRESS

re: Reference/Account/Policy/Membership/Licence No:..

This is to notify you of my/our change of address as follows:

Date of moving out of the above address:

New address:

New telephone no:

Date of moving in:

Would you please amend your records accordingly.

Thank you.

Yours faithfully ....

NOTIFICATION OF CHANGE OF ADDRESS

From:
Address:

Telephone no:

Date:

To:
Address:

Dear Sir/Madam,

NOTIFICATION OF CHANGE OF ADDRESS

re: Reference/Account/Policy/Membership/Licence No:...

This is to notify you of my/our change of address as follows:

Date of moving out of the above address:

New address:

New telephone no:

Date of moving in:

Would you please amend your records accordingly.

Thank you.

Yours faithfully ....

NOTIFICATION OF CHANGE OF ADDRESS

From:
Address:

Telephone no:

Date:

To:
Address:

Dear Sir/Madam,

NOTIFICATION OF CHANGE OF ADDRESS

re: Reference/Account/Policy/Membership/Licence No:...

This is to notify you of my/our change of address as follows:

Date of moving out of the above address:

New address:

New telephone no:

Date of moving in:

Would you please amend your records accordingly.

Thank you.

Yours faithfully ....

NOTIFICATION OF CHANGE OF ADDRESS

From:
Address:

Telephone no:

Date:

To:
Address:

Dear Sir/Madam,

NOTIFICATION OF CHANGE OF ADDRESS

re: Reference/Account/Policy/Membership/Licence No:..

This is to notify you of my/our change of address as follows:

Date of moving out of the above address:

New address:

New telephone no:

Date of moving in:

Would you please amend your records accordingly.

Thank you.

Yours faithfully ....

NOTIFICATION OF CHANGE OF ADDRESS

From:
Address:

Telephone no:

Date:

To:
Address:

Dear Sir/Madam,

NOTIFICATION OF CHANGE OF ADDRESS

re: Reference/Account/Policy/Membership/Licence No:..

This is to notify you of my/our change of address as follows:

Date of moving out of the above address:

New address:

New telephone no:

Date of moving in:

Would you please amend your records accordingly.

Thank you.

Yours faithfully ....